UFOs
The greatest mystery

Hilary Evans

 Albany Books

Designed and produced by
Albany Books
36 Park Street London W1Y 4DE

First published 1979

Published by Albany Books

Printed in Hong Kong

The author gratefully acknowledges the publishers of *Flying
Saucer Review* (SFR Publications, West Malling, Kent,
England) who supplied much of the reference material for the
artwork in this book

Design: Ann Houlgate

Endpapers: *Artist's impression of UFO seen over
Helena, Montana, USA. (Galaxy Search, Mary Evans
Picture Library)*

Previous page: Strangers from the Skies. *(Angus McKie,
Young Artists)*

Right: *A scene from Columbia Pictures'* Close
Encounters of the Third Kind. *(Kobal Collection)*

Contents

The greatest mystery

SIGHTING A UFO

It came in the night,
All shining bright.
The thing let out a blinding glow,
It seemed to have nowhere to go.

Hovering slowly, it seemed to say,
Go away little girl, go away.
The glow turned red, then blue and green.
This is something I wish I hadn't seen.

(Poem by Deborah Stone, age 11, of John Ball School, London)

At any moment — *this* moment, even — you could look out of your window and see a UFO. Perhaps a row of pulsing lights in the night sky, hovering still — as no conventional aircraft can do — then streaking abruptly away — as no helicopter or balloon can do. Perhaps a metallic-looking object, shaped like a disc, cone or cigar, flying low over your car as you drive this afternoon and perhaps even making its motor cut out. Perhaps even parked beside the road or outside your house, its occupants busy around it in some mysterious activity — or even knocking at your door.

It is not easy to believe. But such things have been reported by tens, perhaps hundreds of thousands of people, as normal as you or I. Most of them have given their names and addresses; you could phone them up, here and now, and ask them, is it true, did you really see it, was it really the way you said it was? There are books about UFOs — this is only one of many hundreds — periodicals devoted to them and societies which study them.

There is no doubt about it that UFOs exist — as a phenomenon. But do they exist as a tangible reality? If they do, they are about the most remarkable thing ever experienced by the human race. The sheer size and implications of the UFO phenomenon make the problem almost too big to grasp, which is perhaps why so many people — including scientists and government officials who

ought to know better — turn their faces and refuse to admit that a UFO problem even exists.

Just under a century ago, H. G. Wells wrote *War of the Worlds*, in which he described how our Earth was taken by surprise by invading extraterrestrials. Are we today being taken by surprise in the same way — except that now it is fact rather than fiction? For it is a *fact* that at least half a million people, over a period of some thirty years and more, have reported remarkable objects in the sky. They come from all parts of the world and from all walks of life, many of them being highly qualified scientists, experienced airline pilots, policemen and radar operators. If most of them have been ordinary people, that is because most people *are* ordinary. Only a tiny few have been seeking notoriety or financial gain: apart from those few, most observers have shunned publicity. Over and over again, reading their reports, one is struck by the obvious sincerity of people who, despite inconvenience and the risk of ridicule, have thought it their duty to inform the authorities of what they have seen.

Persistent enigma

But what *is* going on? Perhaps the most baffling aspect of the mystery is that, during the thirty years that investigators have grappled with the UFO problem, the problem has grown, rather than shrunk, in its complexity and size. Someone comes up with an explanation: the next sighting has some feature which shows that that explanation cannot be right — and so it goes on, growing more frustrating all the time. Perhaps it is not surprising that so many people have refused to take them seriously, or have worked so hard to dismiss the entire body of evidence as illusion or fraud.

But the UFO problem will not go away. You can ignore it if you like, as Wells' earthfolk ignored the possibility of a Martian invasion. You can choose, if you will, to believe that there is a natural explanation for every sighting, or that poor observation or deliberate deceit will account for them: but if so, you will have to totally ignore the ever-growing pile of evidence.

This short survey can present only some of that evidence. It is taken from the best-witnessed and most thoroughly checked and investigated of the thousands of reported cases. After making their thorough on-the-spot investigation of a series of cases, including the amazing Kelly case (see pages 62 & 63), a hard-headed American team was forced to conclude:

The almost unavoidable conclusion was that the witnesses in many of these encounters were reporting real events as they perceived them, and that these events described beings who could in no way be confused with any living creatures native to earth.

It will be up to you to decide, after reading what follows, whether you will ignore the UFO problem, or recognise it as the most baffling mystery to confront mankind.

Below: *UFO, ball lightning or camera shake? Photograph taken by Roy Jennings in Castleford, England, at 2 am in August 1961. (Frank Lane)*

Three thousand years of UFOs?

Strange things in the sky have been reported throughout recorded history: but then so have strange things on land — from fairies to Abominable Snowmen — and from the sea — mermaids and sea serpents. Even in our scientific age there are a great many things we cannot account for in terms of present knowledge: in the childhood of mankind, the entire universe was made up of mysteries.

Even then, man sought for explanations instead of just accepting things as they are. He created a parallel world, and peopled it with superhuman beings, to account for what he could not understand — gods of thunder and ocean, goddesses of harvest and death, nymphs of the streams and woods. As his knowledge increased, he found he could manage without the Gods of Olympus; but because there were still many smaller mysteries, he retained his belief in witches and demons, magicians and spirits of the dead.

Tantalisingly, while man's increasing knowledge solved his existing problems one by one, his continual curiosity kept finding more problems demanding a solution. As it became easier for him to travel across his planet, he found traces of very strange things, things hard to explain in terms of his existing knowledge: the strange markings of the Nazca Lines in Peru, which seem to make sense only when seen from the air; the baffling architecture of the Pyramids; the riddle of the Easter Island carvings; and the stone alignments of Carnac in Brittany — these are just a few of the archaeological problems which continue to baffle the scholar.

In search of an explanation, man turned to written records preserved by other cultures: there he found references to gods who visited the earth and travelled in airborne chariots. The consequence has been a vast new literary industry of speculation about early man. Some of it has been soundly based and has led to important re-evaluations of our ancestors, particularly with regard to the amount of skill and knowledge that they possessed. But alongside this solid research has been a vast structure of speculation that our earth has

been visited periodically throughout history by extraterrestrial beings from superior cultures. UFOs, it is suggested, are only the latest manifestation in a continuing saga of interplanetary visitation.

It is impossible to summarize all the relevant literature here but, insofar as it affects our study of the UFO phenomenon, we must consider whether it has a useful contribution to make. On the basis of the evidence hitherto presented, the answer to that must be a regretful negative.

The archaeological evidence for early extraterrestrial visitation is very limited in extent, and totally inconclusive. There are indeed some strange artifacts lying about in the jungles of South America: but there is not the slightest reason to presuppose any form of celestial origin. Alleged

Below: *Not astronauts but gods. The Indian deity Brahma and his suite watch the fighting between Arjuna and Karna. (British Museum, Michael Holford Library)*

Above: *Fresco, c. 6000 BC, from Tassili, Sahara Desert, seen by some as depicting an extraterrestrial space traveller, but almost certainly a neolithic representation of a ritually masked celebrant. (Fortean Picture Library)*

UFOs of the past?

Thousands of references have been found in the mythology of various cultures which could — just conceivably — refer to UFOs. Here is just a small sampling:

332 BC. While Alexander the Great was besieging Tyre, 'Flying Shields' appeared over the Greek camp — round discs, flying in triangular formation, one larger than the others by about a half. For a while both armies watched amazed: then from the leader came flashes directed at the city's defences, causing walls and towers to crumble as if built of mud. The besieging army poured in: the discs hovered overhead till the city had been successfully taken, then swiftly climbed into the sky and vanished.

66 BC. Pliny the historian tells how at Rome, during the consulship of Gnaeus Octavius and Gaius Scribonius, a spark was seen to fall from a star. It increased in size as it approached the earth till it was as large as the moon. For a while it stood in the sky, diffusing a sort of cloudy daylight; then it returned into the sky, taking the shape of a torch as it did so.

1661. A Belgian Jesuit missionary in Tibet, Albert d'Orville, saw a flying object shaped like a double Chinese conical hat: silently, it circled the city twice, then, surrounded by mist, vanished. A lama told d'Orville that it was the vehicle of beings who sail the seas of Space and have brought enlightened teachings to mankind in the past, and that these beings continued to visit the monasteries of Tibet, teaching and revealing lost knowledge.

1792. On 18 June a luminous object, as large as a bamboo hut, was seen flying over Yedo at about 11pm: it was so bright that it lit up the entire countryside.

1976. Robert Temple, in *The Sirius Mystery*, examines and substantiates the report that the Dogon of Mali, a primitive tribe of central Africa, have known for more than a century that Sirius has two satellites, which move in a particular way; these details have only recently been established by astronomers with the aid of modern technology.

Right: *Alexander's celestial journey. Some claim this Muhgal manuscript as evidence that Indians in medieval times had mastered flight. For others it is a splendidly imaginative myth. (British Museum, Michael Holford Library)*

portrayals of space visitors by primitive artists can easily be given alternative explanations. To see a UFO-shaped inscription on an undeciphered Cretan tablet does not prove that the Minoan civilisation was visited from space.

The written records—the testimony of mythology — while undoubtedly of the greatest interest, are equally inconclusive. Even if we yield so far as to say that there is good evidence that some early human cultures had to some degree mastered flight, that would still not imply that the secret was taught them by beings from other worlds.

So, while such theories are almost impossible to disprove, we must face the fact that they are based on the flimsiest of evidence, often manipulated in a most unscholarly manner. Let us by all means keep an open mind on the subject and admit the possibility of extraterrestrial visitation. But let us not look to these theorists for any useful help in our very real problem of understanding UFOs in the twentieth-century skies.

Six shades of strangeness

UFO experiences take several different forms, ranging from the simple sighting of something strange in the sky to extended personal encounters with UFO occupants. Some of the first group can — though often only with difficulty — be 'explained' by scientists; but the more complex cases can be dismissed only by accusing the percipient of downright lying.

1 Lights

Usually seen at night, this is the most frequently reported type of sighting. You may see a single light, a row of lights, or a number of separate lights. They may be white or coloured, or they may change colour. A big light may fragment into smaller lights, separate lights may join to form one large one. They may remain still, or move purposefully, or move apparently meaninglessly. Many natural objects can, under particular circumstances, behave very strangely, so sceptics may be right in ascribing many of these sightings to natural phenomena such as the reflections of city lights on clouds or even on migrating birds. But though lights on their own must be the least satisfactory form of sighting, it is hard to believe that *every* one is a passing goose, or the planet Venus, or a car headlamp on a distant hill.

2 Shapes

At night it is usually impossible to see anything but lights, but sometimes, if the sky is starlit, or at dusk or dawn, a looming shape may be discerned. Most often, though, shaped UFOs are seen during daylight. As will be seen, the range of possible shapes is almost infinite, which means that experts trying to explain them away have to dream up an equally wide variety of objects for which they may be mistaken. No doubt many sightings are indeed aircraft in unusual conditions, or balloons or clouds: but most of us know such objects when we see them — and know that a sharp-edged metallic-looking object, moving soundlessly, making abrupt right-angle turns and moving away at speeds faster than any aircraft can achieve, is something else again.

3 Radar observations

Radar operators employed by government departments are of necessity highly trained, as it is on their expertise that the security of their country depends. Radar can, under unusual circumstances, behave abnormally; but it is a vital part of radar training to recognise these erratic manifestations when they occur. So when a radar operator reports the sighting of an object moving at an incredible speed, vanishing and reappearing without cause, and behaving in a way beyond the capability of any known aircraft, he usually knows what he is talking about. This is of course especially true when his observation is confirmed by visual sighting, as has happened on many occasions.

4 Contact cases

The simplest kind of contact case consists of some sort of distant interaction between a UFO and the earth. For example, a UFO may show apparent interest in a car or a farm tractor, and hover over the vehicle in a way which seems to suggest that it is inspecting it. No occupants may be seen: conscious control is deduced only from the way the UFO behaves, so that the possibility of remote control cannot be ruled out. There are many cases in which aircraft have been shadowed by UFOs, often over long distances, with no action on the UFO's part other than the mere act of accompanying. Simple curiosity, or what?

5 Encounters

In an encounter case, personal contact is alleged between the percipient and UFO occupant(s). In almost every reported case, this is a matter of an unaccompanied person's experience, which of course increases our suspicion, though there is a possible explanation that the UFO occupant may not wish to confront more than one earthperson. In such reports, the occupants are usually able to communicate, either in the percipient's own language or by telepathy. They are generally more or less human in appearance and behaviour, and are usually described as 'humanoids'. Many commentators who accept UFOs in themselves are sceptical about their occupants — and yet at least some of the evidence is, as we shall see, quite as good as much that is accepted in a court of law.

6 Boardings

Sometimes the encounter happens to go further: the percipient is taken — usually by invitation but sometimes by force, though this is generally mental rather than physical   on board the UFO. This is usually described as being for the purpose of physical examination, the earthpersons being made to lie on a table while they are probed and prodded by alien 'doctors'. The luckier ones are then taken on a conducted tour of the vehicle, and even for a flight which may well include a visit to remote planets. It would be tempting to dismiss all such reports as coming from the imagination, but some of the information communicated to the percipients has a compelling logic to it which makes it hard for us to be totally sceptical.

Below: *David Jackson, Young Artists.*

Case History:

The Socorro sighting

CATEGORY:	Contact (remote)
PLACE:	Socorro, New Mexico, USA
DATE:	24 April 1964
TIME:	19.50 hrs, full daylight
WEATHER:	Fine, clear, some light cloud
PERCIPIENT:	Lonnie Zamora, age 31, police officer, five years experience

Zamora was in his patrol car, chasing a speeder on the road leading out of town, when he heard a roar and saw a tall 'cone of flame', blue-orange in colour, about 825m (900yd) into the desert, near where he knew an explosives store was located. Considering the risk of an explosion more important than his speeder, he turned his car in that direction, leaving the main road and turning down a dirt track which crossed an area of low hills.

He lost sight of the light as he climbed a low hill: when he reached the top there was nothing to be seen or heard. Then he saw what had to be the-source of the 'explosion' — a whitish metallic-looking object down in a ravine, about 140-180m (150-200yd) from him. He stopped to observe it more clearly:

> At first I wanted to think it looked like a white car turned over maybe on its side, with the far end somehow higher than the nearer one. But that didn't seem right, the way it looked. . . . Then I saw two small figures in what resembled white coveralls, pretty close to the object, as if inspecting it. . . . One of the figures seemed to turn as if it heard or saw my car coming. It must have seen me, 'cause when it turned and looked straight at my car, it seemed startled — almost seemed to jump somewhat.

He decided to try for a closer look and drove on towards what looked like a good vantage point. This involved going down a dip in the road, so losing sight of the object; as he went he radioed for another police officer to join him as soon as possible, though describing it simply as an accident. He was still talking as he brought his car to the edge of the ravine where he had seen the object: now he could see it below him, at a distance of 15-30m (50-100ft). As he bent to replace his microphone he heard a slamming sound, and when he looked up again the two figures had disappeared.

Zamora left the car and started to walk down the slope towards the object, but had only gone about three paces when he 'heard a sudden, very loud, car-splitting roar; the noise and flame came on'. Anticipating an explosion, he turned and started to run back towards the car, then threw himself down on the ground, losing his glasses in the process. The roaring sound continued but no explosion occurred, so he got up and continued running, watching back over his shoulder, until he was the far side of the car and could use it as a shield. He saw the object rise to the level of his car, taking about six seconds to do so. Then the roar ceased and the object started to move away in absolute silence, skimming close to the ground. About 1600m (1700yd) away it angled up at a steep climb and vanished rapidly.

Nobody else saw the object so vividly as Zamora, but several other witnesses confirmed the strange light. When his colleagues arrived, they found indications that an object had been standing where he said it had, and there were signs that the scrub had been burned in the same area.

The Socorro sighting is one of the most thoroughly investigated of all UFO cases, and though it depends almost wholly on the testimony of one percipient, it stands as one of the classic sightings. Either Zamora is lying, or he was mistaken. If he made the whole thing up, we still have to explain what the strange flame was that the other witnesses saw. If he was merely mistaken in what he saw, we have to ask ourselves why he would continue to insist that he saw something which bore no resemblance to a helicopter or other conventional aircraft, and to report behaviour beyond the capability of any known vehicle. Zamora's story will be found easier to believe when it is compared with other reported sightings.

Right: John Gosler

Case History:

The Lakenheath sightings

CATEGORY:	Radar, lights
PLACE:	Lakenheath, near Cambridge, England
DATE:	13-14 August 1956
TIME:	21.30-02.30 hrs
PERCIPIENTS:	RAF & USAF radar and ground personnel

The Lakenheath sightings lasted over a period of five hours, during which time they were observed visually from the ground and air and by ground and airborne radar, often simultaneously. Despite strict investigation, no satisfactory natural explanation has been forthcoming.

1 21.30 hrs. Radar at Bentwaters RAF station picks up object heading NW from point ESE of Bentwaters, travelling at 6500-14,500kph (4000-9000mph) and tracks it for 30 seconds.

2 Minutes later. Same radar picks up three objects in triangular formation, separated by at least 300m (1000ft), followed by about twelve others scattered irregularly over a larger area, moving at 130-200kph (80-125mph). After being tracked for 25 minutes, all converge to form one signal several times larger than a bomber. Object remains stationary for 10-15 minutes, then moves on, stops again, moves and vanishes. T-33 fighter asked to check: no contact.

3 22.00 hrs. Radar spots another object 50km (30 miles) east, moving at 6500-20,000kph (4000-12,000mph). Seconds later, ground personnel see UFO in form of light moving without a sound at very high speed: simultaneously radar picks up object passing overhead and C-47 aircraft, flying overhead, sees light *below* it. As C-47 is flying at 1200m (4000ft), UFO's altitude is estimated at 600-900m (2000-3000ft). UFO disappears to west. In view of direction of UFO's path, Bentwaters alerts Lakenheath airfield, WNW of Bentwaters. Lakenheath reports visual sighting, but discrepancies of direction and altitude make identification with Bentwaters UFO

purely conjectural. Lakenheath object is low-flying luminous object coming from northeast, which stops then moves on.

4 Later, ground observers at Lakenheath see two moving white lights which appear to merge and vanish together; report describes them as moving 'at terrific speeds and then stopping and changing course immediately'. Both speed and course changes are confirmed by two sets of radar of two different types, making chance that both are malfunctioning simultaneously and in a similar manner virtually negligible. Ground observer estimates size as equivalent to golf ball held at arm's length.

5 About 24.00 hrs. RAF *Venom* jet with nose radar is sent up from Waterbeach RAF base, 35km (20 miles) southwest of Lakenheath. As it comes over Lakenheath, radar there picks up UFO and *Venom* is directed to intercept. Pilot sees bright white light, obtains radar confirmation, chases and loses it.

6 Lakenheath, monitoring another UFO on ground radar, directs *Venom* to intercept it. Again, airborne radar confirms. Ground radar watches while *Venom* loses UFO but UFO starts to chase *Venom,* which tries to shake loose but fails. Ground radar registers two distinct targets, implying a separation of 60-180m (200-600ft).

7 After some ten minutes, *Venom* has to return to base for refuelling. UFO follows for a distance, then vanishes. Second *Venom* is sent up, sees nothing and has to return due to engine fault.

This case, in which all the witnesses are airforce personnel whose expertise is not in question, and where a majority of the sightings are confirmed, some of them twice over, stands as one of the most firmly established of all UFO sightings. The only conceivable explanation is that flying objects, under purposeful control and capable of speeds and manoeuvres substantially in excess of any known aircraft, were in the skies over Lakenheath on that August night.

Right: *Peter Jones, Artist Partners*

Case History:

The Papua sighting

CATEGORY:	Contact, (remote)
PLACE:	Papua, New Guinea
DATE:	26 and 27 June 1959
TIME:	After sunset, both evenings, for some hours
WEATHER:	Clear evening sky
PERCIPIENTS:	William Gill, age 31, Australian Anglican missionary, together with 37 other witnesses

Father Gill's Mission is located on an isolated part of the Pacific island of Papua; the Mission House is surrounded by coconut palms and other trees and overlooks the beach. Father Gill had just finished his evening meal, and stepped outside his Mission House to look at the evening sky. Glancing up, he reported: 'I saw Venus, but I also saw this sparkling object which was very, very bright. I saw it descend towards us.' It came down to 90-120m (300-400ft) and he compared its width to that of a hand held at arm's length. Far off it seemed a brilliant white, then this changed to a dull yellow and finally a pale orange colour.

All witnesses agreed that the object looked solid, was circular, with a wide base and a narrower upper deck, and had legs. They were not all in agreement about details, but most claimed to see portholes or windows in the side: Father Gill himself saw what looked like panels, but not necessarily windows. The object sent up intermittent shafts of blue light into the sky at angles of about 45°.

> As we watched it, men came out from the object, and appeared on the top of it, on what seemed to be a deck on top of the huge disc. There were four men in all, occasionally two, then one, three, four . . . the men appeared to be illuminated by a sort of glow which completely surrounded them as well as the craft.

Though the witnesses were not close enough to make out any details, they appeared to be more or less human in form. There was never any sound.

After nearly half an hour the object left, but it returned about an hour later, though not so closely this time and there was no sign of the men. It stayed there for some two and a half hours, during which time other, smaller lights were also seen in the sky, moving erratically. It was seen altogether by thirty eight witnesses, including five teachers and three medical assistants.

The following evening the object reappeared, slightly earlier in the evening, just after sunset, while it was still quite light. Again, four figures appeared, one of them seeming to be leaning on a rail as if it had been a ship. 'I stretched my arm above my head and waved. To our surprise the figure did the same. Others waved and got answering waves. There seemed to be no doubt that our movements were answered.' When a torch was flashed, the UFO seemed to make movements like a pendulum in response. Though the watchers shouted up, there was no audible reply.

At 6.30 pm Father Gill went in to dinner — an item of behaviour which has surprised some commentators who forget how long the sighting lasted. When he came out again at about 7 pm the object was still there, but there was no sign of the occupants. Then he went to church: after the service, there was no sign of the object. Later that evening a terrific explosion was heard though nothing was seen. Its connection with the sighting was perhaps only a coincidence, but it was enough to make Father Gill, accustomed though he was to the thunderstorms of the region, jump out of bed.

Papua seems to have had more than its share of sightings. The Father Gill case, though the best reported, is only one of 79 reported UFO sightings spread over five years. Others were witnessed by many percipients in responsible positions, including clergymen, government officials, the manager of an airline and the head of the Department of Civil Aviation. Confirmed by such a weight of testimony, there seems little doubt that Papua is a major centre of UFO activity: the next question is, Why?

Right: *Terry Hadler, Young Artists*

In search of hard evidence

Socorro, Lakenheath, Papua. Just three cases taken from hundreds equally remarkable, in which people we have no reason to disbelieve have made a persuasive claim that we have no reason to doubt — except that we cannot quite bring ourselves to believe. If these people saw what they said they saw, then these objects, whatever they are, must surely be the most remarkable phenomena ever reported by anyone, anywhere, at any time. Why is it, then, that neither governments nor academic establishments officially recognise their existence? Why is it that the only investigations worthy of the name are carried out by ordinary men and women, volunteers, with no support or encouragement from those established authorities which normally look into every strange phenomenon, from the stars in the heavens to life on the ocean floor? To this question there are several possible answers.

They just don't want to know

Could it be that governments are scared of the implications of UFOs and hope that they will vanish as mysteriously as they arrived? While such a theory might be true of individuals, it is hardly likely to hold good of corporate bodies, whether it is a government department or an academic institution.

They don't know and they don't care

According to this theory, the authorities regard all those who see UFOs, and all who take them seriously, as deluded; for them there is no UFO problem, so why should it be given the privilege of official notice? There are better ways of spending the taxpayer's money and better ways of utilising the expert's time. But, while it must be confessed that the lunatic fringe in ufology is both conspicuous and vociferous, it is equally true that there is an overwhelming quantity of serious testimony. Anyone who makes any kind of objective study must see that a UFO problem — of some sort — exists, and that governments have a responsibility to check that problem out.

They are interested — but they're keeping quiet about it

Those who find official silence hard to believe have formulated a variety of theories, all based on the thesis that governments are in fact taking a very serious interest in UFOs, but keeping that interest quiet for reasons of their own. We shall be looking at the 'conspiracy' theory later on, and noting that in America at least, both the CIA and FBI have undoubtedly been involved. There is, however, no necessity to presuppose any sinister intention. Perhaps it is simply that the authorities, baffled by the UFO, are reluctant to admit their failure to understand it on the grounds that this might create public panic. So, until they do discover what UFOs are, they prefer to keep their involvement quiet.

They know there's a problem — but they don't know what kind of problem it is

A variation on the previous suggestion — and perhaps now we are getting close to the true state of the matter. Is the UFO a problem for the astronomer, for the military, for the engineer, for the psychiatrist or for the psychical researcher?

Confronted by so fundamental a dilemma, it would seem that the obvious thing to do would be to form an inter-disciplinary study group, so that expertise could be shared. In practice, just the opposite has taken place: each group of experts has ducked the issue and looked for someone else to pass the buck to.

A shameful state of things? Yes, but each dodger has his excuse. The astronomer protests that he spends his life watching the skies — if UFOs exist, surely he would see a dozen every night? The engineer works with structures and components: give him a single nut or bolt from a certified UFO, and he'll set to work with a will. The same kind of reaction appears with each of the experts in whose province the UFO may legitimately belong.

The dismaying fact is that there is not a scrap of hard evidence for the UFO — only tens of thousands of reports, describing what people claim to have seen. It may be objected that the same is true of the planet Venus, which everyone has seen but nobody has actually touched; but at least all the observations of Venus tend to corroborate one another. By contrast the UFO appears in a different shape, size and form almost every time it's seen; behaves differently on almost every occasion; is maddeningly elusive and totally unpredictable.

Below: *In the absence of any official investigation, the task has fallen to amateurs. But that does not imply any lack of expertise: scientists and engineers, doctors and psychiatrists, are among the professionals whose skill has been harnessed to the attempt to meet the UFO challenge. Their findings are published in journals throughout the world. The most authoritative is* The Flying Saucer Review, *published in Britain, which for a quarter of a century has sought to document the UFO problem in all its complexity. (Mary Evans Picture Library)*

The evidence of the camera

In the regrettable absence of a nuts-and-bolts UFO for the engineer to examine with his calipers and sliderule, the next best kind of evidence should be that provided by the camera. Thousands of UFO photographs exist, including several films. Yet it remains true that not a single one, from all those thousands, is wholly convincing. The witness may be of unshakeable integrity and experts may assure us that the negative reveals no sign of tampering. But UFO photos continue to show us an object too small for analysis; or blurred with movement; or out of focus; or with no frame of reference to establish size and distance. None of which necessarily means that the pictures are fraudulent: just that they cannot be accepted as certain proof.

Explanations are not hard to find. Few of us carry a camera at all times — though with modern pocket cameras there is no reason why we shouldn't — and, if we do, the excitement of seeing a UFO is liable to cause confusion in which it is easy to forget to adjust the camera properly. Most UFOs are seen at night, when photography is difficult if not impossible; or, if in daylight, at a very great distance where all that is captured is a distant speck of light. If they are seen more closely, they are apt to move rapidly and erratically enough to frustrate even the most professional photographer. And even if a close-up *is* achieved, it will be blurred in outline, hazy in detail, caused — so the UFO believer will tell you — by the 'force field' which surrounds the vehicle.

Some day soon, perhaps some lucky photographer will give us the evidence we so desperately need. Until then, as the examples on these pages show only too well, the photographic evidence is tantalisingly thin.

Below: *UFO photographed in the Bernina Mountains, Italy, by engineer Giampiero Monguzzi on 31 July 1952. (Flying Saucer Review)*

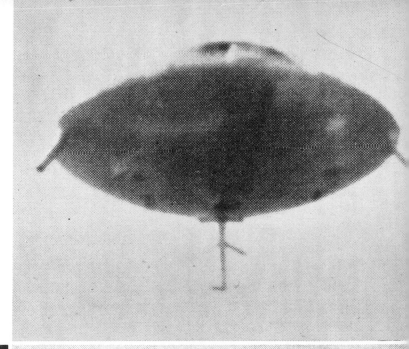

Right: *The best of the fake photographs, created by Radio Officer Fogl in 1957, revealed as a hoax nine years later. (Flying Saucer Review)*

Middle left: *UFO photographed by Ella Fortune over Holloman Air Force Base, Alamogordo, New Mexico, on 10 October 1957. (Fortean Picture Library)*

Middle right: *UFOs photographed by Stephen Pratt at Conisborough, England, on 28 March 1966. (Fortean Picture Library)*

Bottom left: *UFO photographed over Coniston, England, by schoolboy Stephen Darbishire, on 15 February 1954. (Fortean Picture Library)*

Bottom right: *UFO photographed over Venezuela by Avena Airlines pilot flying between Barcelona and Miquetia in 1963. The relative positions of shadows to objects and aircraft, not seen in this photograph, made this almost certainly a fake. (Fortean Picture Library)*

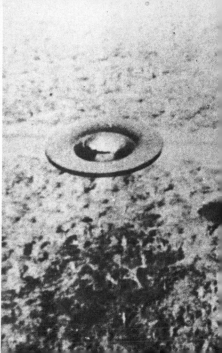

Natural causes

Before an investigator classifies an alleged sighting as a true UFO experience, he will first satisfy himself that there is not a simpler explanation; which means, most often, a natural explanation. Astronomers and meteorologists, professionally aware of the astonishing forms that natural phenomena can assume, have always been inclined to regard all UFO sightings as being capable of a natural explanation: some, such as the late Professor Menzel of Harvard who wrote three books and gave countless lectures on the subject, have made determined — some would say, hysterical — efforts to explain away *all* UFO reports. In so doing, they have done the ufologists a service, for the fact that, after all their efforts, a substantial number of UFO reports remain unexplained, is the surest possible evidence of their reality.

Certainly some of the things that nature can get up to verge on the incredible. Venus can look unnaturally large; mock suns can appear beside the real one; temperature inversions can cause a variety of optical phenomena in the sky; winds can carve clouds into shapes which take on the appearance of artifacts. Other phenomena, such as ball lightning, are so rare and extraordinary that even many scientists do not believe in their existence!

When the United States Air Force was officially investigating UFOs it employed Dr Allen Hynek, a professional astronomer, as its consultant. Today he confesses: 'I too thought at the time that UFOs were just a lot of nonsense. I enjoyed the role of debunker.' But in his report of 30 April 1949 he and his colleagues found that only 32% of the sightings investigated could be attributed to astronomical causes. 12% were thought to be balloons and 33% were either misidentified aircraft, or hoaxes, or lacked sufficient data for evaluation. This left 23% which could not be explained.

23% of many thousands of reports means a great number of unexplained objects moving about in our skies. Speaking later to the American Association for the Advancement of Science in December 1969. Dr Hynek declared:

> My twenty-one years of monitoring of UFO reports has shown that a large number are readily identifiable by trained investigators as misperception of known objects and events. A small residue of UFO reports are not so identifiable. . . . Although I know of no hypothesis that adequately covers the mountainous evidence, this should not deter us from following the advice of Schroedinger: to be curious, capable of being astonished, and eager to find out.

Top left: *Horizontal moon. From Blunt,* Beauty of the Heavens, *1849. (Mary Evans Picture Library)*

Left: *Zodiacal light. From* Beauty of the Heavens.

Top left: *Annular eclipse of the sun. From* Beauty of the Heavens.

Top middle: *Meteor. From* Beauty of the Heavens.

Top right: *Total solar eclipse observed from Tarragona, Spain, in 1860. From* Agnes Giberne, Sun, Moon and Stars. *(Ann Ronan Picture Library)*

Middle left: *Parhelion. From* Beauty of the Heavens.

Middle right: *Cirro-cumulus clouds. From* Beauty of the Heavens.

Right: *Parhelia. From* Beauty of the Heavens.

The prophets:
Jules Verne and H·G·Wells

Whatever man can imagine, he will construct tales about. For as long as he has been aware of the stars, he has created myths and legends about them — picturing people dwelling on them, imagining them coming to our earth or earthmen going there.

But myth is a very different thing from serious fiction, which tends to be only one step in advance of scientific progress. It was only when man had achieved flight within his own atmosphere that writers began to explore in their imaginations the possibility of spaceflight as a practicable venture.

Jules Verne's *From the Earth to the Moon* of 1865, with its sequel *Round the Moon* published five years later, was a staggering feat of the imagination. True, it was naive in its technology: Verne pictured the rocket being fired from an enormous gun. We know that idea to be unworkable, but Verne could not have known that. In almost every other respect, his account was logical and acutely reasoned, anticipating many developments of modern spaceflight, such as the fact that rockets would be required to modify the course of the spacecraft during flight.

As a writer, Verne was naive and pedestrian; his great merit lay in the sheer force of his ideas. His successor, H. G. Wells, combined rich imagination with an astonishing flair for story-telling. *The War of the Worlds* of 1890 opens with a rivetting paragraph calculated to grip the most casual reader:

> No one would have believed, in the last years of the nineteenth century, that human affairs were being watched keenly and closely by intelligences greater than man's and yet as mortal as his own; that as men busied themselves about their affairs they were scrutinised and studied, perhaps almost as narrowly as a man with a microscope might scrutinise the transient creatures that swarm and multiply in a drop of water. . . . Yet, across the gulf of space, minds that were to our minds as ours are to those of the beasts that perish, intellects vast and cool and unsympathetic, regarded this earth with envious eyes, and slowly and surely drew their plans against us. . . .

In a later book, *The First Men in the Moon,* Wells, too, sent his travellers to Earth's nearest neighbour in space. With more practical information than Verne had had, he realised that no gun would do the job of overcoming gravity: so he had his inventor Cavor create an anti-gravity substance. But Wells is concerned less with the nuts-and-bolts of spaceflight than with the problems created by man's contact with extraterrestrial creatures: as in *The War of the Worlds,* what interests him is the confrontation between two alien civilisations, an issue equally central to the present UFO problem.

Following in the steps of Verne and Wells came many other writers, most mere imitators but some with worthwhile contributions of their own. But more significantly, these authors were overtaken by the inventors. The year after *The First Men in the Moon* was published, the Wright brothers successfully capped the Montgolfiers' achievement by solving the problem of *powered* flight. Now at last man could start to control the sky above his head: fact was catching up with fiction.

Right: *The Martians advance on the Thames. Illustration by Warwick Goble for H. G. Wells'* The War of the Worlds, *1890. (Mary Evans Picture Library)*

Below: *The projectile in space, accompanied by ejected objects. From Jules Verne,* Round the Moon, *1870. (Mary Evans Picture Library)*

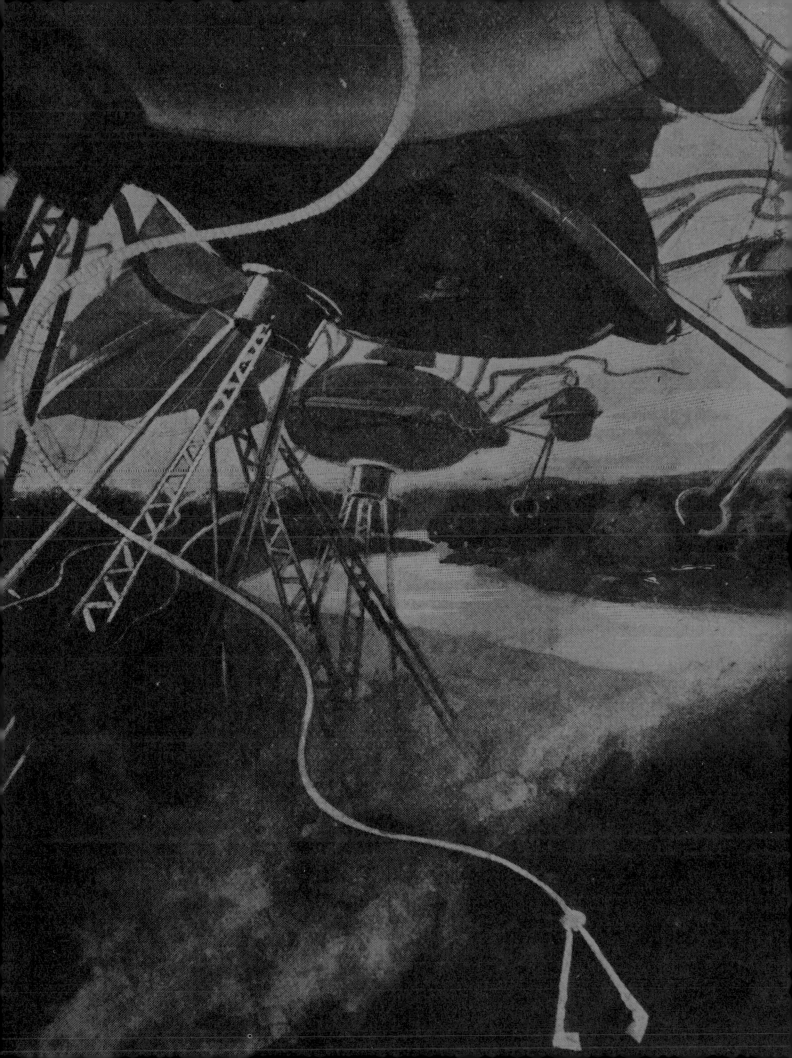

The American airships of 1897

CATEGORY:	Various, including encounter
PLACE:	Many parts of USA, chiefly mid-west
DATE:	Mainly March-April 1897
PERCIPIENTS:	Many hundreds, including multiple sightings

In June 1900 Count von Zeppelin's first airship just made it into the air over Lake Constance and succeeded in staying up for seventeen uncertain minutes. That first tentative flight is hailed today as the epoch-making start of powered flight: yet if we can believe the accounts, three years before that date there were airships that cruised the skies of America at will, travelling great distances at high speed, at leisure and in comfort.

Absurd? Yet the reports can be read in the news-papers of the day, adding up to so substantial a volume of testimony that we must either believe that several hundred sober and respected American citizens, of all ages and walks of life, widely scattered and quite unknown to one another, were united in some vast and meaningless conspiracy to delude their fellow citizens; or that they were all suffering from a shared hallucination, unknown to one another though they might be; or that there really were airships, more advanced than any flying machine of the day, touring the American skies in 1897.

Here, for example, is what the citizens of Everest, Kansas, saw for 80 minutes on the night of 1 April (if that date is significant, then the same joke was being played in many other parts of the country that same night):

> The outlines were clearly distinguished. The basket or car seemed to be 25 to 30 feet [7.5 to 9m] long, shaped like an Indian canoe. Four light wings extended from the car, two were triangular. A large dark bulk was discernible immediately above the car and was generally supposed to be an inflated gasbag. The power-ful lights on board were reflected on the clouds. That the same power that furnished the light was used for lifting the ship was evident from the fact that the lights grew dim as the ship went upward, and as the ship came nearer the earth, the light was as bright as the light of a locomotive.

As with today's UFO problem, each sighting seemed to be different. Here are details from some other accounts:

1 April, Galesburg, Michigan. Witnesses saw a brilliant light and vaguely made out a dark shape; they heard an odd crackling noise — presumably the motor — and the distinct sounds of human voices.

5 April, Omaha. A cigar-shaped object, with the appearance of steel, was seen flying into the wind at high speed.

9 April, Chicago. A long dark object seen at night, estimated length 21m (70ft), wings about 6m (20ft) wide. One witness claimed that there were two cigar-shaped bodies attached by girders; curiously this improbable description is confirmed by at least one other account.

11 April, Norman, Oklahoma. Nearly 400 people saw a long dark object with a very bright red light on its end and flashing red lights along its sides.

28 April, Dallas. A lawyer saw a 'huge black monster, in shape something like a cigar, but underneath there seemed to be a body similar to the body of a ship; it must have gone at the rate of 100mph [160kph] or more.'

Those who saw the objects never thought that they were anything but native American craft: certainly, no extraterrestrial theories entered their heads. Yet the eminent aeronautical historian, Charles Gibbs-Smith, has authoritatively stated:

> The only airborne vehicles, carrying passen-gers, which could possibly have been seen anywhere in North America in 1897 were free flying spherical balloons, and it is highly unlikely for these to be mistaken for anything

EN L'AN 2000

Above: *An airship of AD 2000 — as predicted in 1900. By an astonishing coincidence, it matches almost perfectly the airship actually reported over Chicago three years earlier. From a card issued by a French chocolate manufacturer. (Mary Evans Picture Library)*

else. No form of dirigible was flying — or could fly — at this time in America.

True, there had been many experiments with airships, notably in France, so it is not improbable that some Americans had thought of doing the same. But there is no record of their even making such an attempt, let alone succeeding; is it conceivable that they could have done so, and kept it secret? Even if an inventor had wanted to thwart his competitors by concealing his success, it is hard to believe that he could have done so for long. That apart, the wide variety of the objects would suggest a great number of separate vehicles, presumably created by separate inventors.

For many commentators, the most significant aspect of the 1897 phenomenon is that it represented a technological development only one step ahead of that which had already been attained — just as, today, the extraterrestrial UFO would seem to be only one generation, technologically speaking, in advance of current achievement. It is argued that what we are experiencing — and what those American percipients in 1897 were experiencing — is some kind of displacement in time. We shall return to this subject later when we have gathered more facts.

The science-fiction age

THE MASTER OF THE WORLD

JULES VERNE

Where Verne and Wells had shown the way, others eagerly followed. In the early years of the twentieth century, encouraged by the successful conquest of controlled flight, speculation ran wild. Fictional explorers used flying machines to carry them to strange lost worlds; criminals used them to carry out daring coups; and while many peaceful applications of flight were envisaged, its potential for warfare was not ignored.

World War I saw these worst fears confirmed when the horrifying possibilities of aerial bombardment became reality. For a while this put a damper on flights of airborne fancy; but by the late 1920s the world was forgetting the horrors of the Western Front and, once again, imaginations began to explore the possibilities of flight. Suddenly the great science-fiction boom was on.

Soon a host of pulp magazines — so named from the cheap paper on which they were printed — were providing writers with the opportunity to let their minds run free: *Amazing Stories, Astounding Stories, Marvel Science Stories* — these and many others, month after month, poured out a flood of fantasy on the earth. By 1928 Hugo Gernsback, editor of *Amazing Stories,* could solemnly declare: 'In our editorial opinion, our modern authors have far eclipsed both Jules Verne and H.G. Wells.'

For the science-fiction writers of the 1930s, as for H.G. Wells forty years earlier, the biggest question

Left: *Cover by J. Roux for the English edition of Jules Verne's* The Master of the World, *1903. (MEPL)*

Right: *Cover by Harold Piffard for F. Hernaman-Johnson's* The Polyphemes, *1906. (MEPL)*

was whether the extraterrestrials would be friendly or hostile. Two illustrations from the July 1939 issue of *Fantastic Adventures* neatly encapsulate the problem. The kindly inhabitants of Venus welcome the visiting Earthman with flipper raised high in friendly greeting, while Venus-mom and Venus-kids stand beaming in the doorway of their home into which the visitors will surely be invited for a friendly drink. When the Sirians land on earth, however, it is with no benevolent intent; those who seek to frustrate their diabolical plan (to steal the Earth, what else?) encounter a ghastly fate:

> His face dark with rage, his tentacled eyes gleaming wickedly, the Sirian lifted his weapon. Between it and Pierson's body shut-

tled a path of gleaming particles of matter. Instantly a change came over the man. Webb gasped as he saw what was happening. He was seeing Pierson as though he were made of jelly! His bones were visible as those of a skeleton. The jelly quivered into nothingness, the bones vanished with the abrupt suddenness of a light that has been turned out. Pierson was gone; a little swirl of dust drifted where he had stood.

Right: *A friendly welcome on the planet Venus. Illustration by Frank R. Paul for* Fantastic Adventures, *1939. (Mary Evans Picture Library)*

Below: *Hostile invaders from Sirius. Illustration by Leo Morey for* Fantastic Adventures, *1939.* (MEPL)

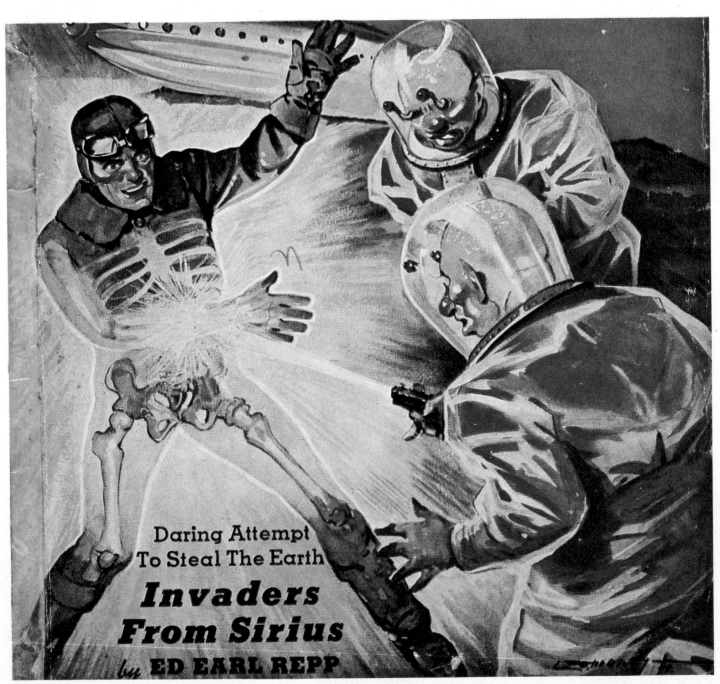

Daring Attempt
To Steal The Earth
**Invaders
From Sirius**
by **ED EARL REPP**

THE MAN FROM VENUS

by **PAUL**

A scientific conception of life on earth's nearest neighbor. Science says Venus is a sister world and human forms of life are more possible than on any other planet.

(For further details see page 97)

Foo Fighters and Ghost Rockets

Foo Fighters

22 December 1944. — At 0600 near Hagenau, at 10,000ft [3000m] altitude, two very bright lights climbed towards us from the ground. They levelled off and stayed on the tail of our plane. They were huge, bright orange lights. They stayed there for two minutes. On my tail all the time. They were under perfect control. Then they turned away from us, and the fire seemed to go out.

What Lieutenant David McFalls, flying with the USAF over Germany during the last year of the war in Europe, was reporting was a 'Foo Fighter' (the name came from *feu,* the French word for fire). The allied fliers who encountered them assumed they were a German secret weapon — they were also known as *krautballs* — but they never attacked aircraft or did any damage. Later the same phenomenon was encountered in the far-eastern sector of the war: Japanese pilots saw them and presumed them to be American in origin while the Americans thought them Japanese.

The first Foo Fighter seems to have been reported in November 1944, after which reports came in quite frequently over a period of months. Then the phenomena suddenly ceased — which makes it difficult to explain them away by finding a natural explanation. The size was variously reported: one seen in that first month was described as 'a hell of a huge, fierce, fiery orange light' which travelled at about 400kph (250mph). Radar, whether from ground or air, picked up nothing on any occasion — another significant if unhelpful fact.

The obvious guess, after discounting the secret weapon suggestion, is that they were some kind of meteorological phenomenon, like ball lightning — an electrical discharge building up briefly into some kind of visible shape. But whereas ball lightning never lasts for more than a few minutes, and generally only two or three seconds, the Foo Fighters were known to persist for prolonged periods — a B29 bomber in the Pacific was followed by a glowing object, about a metre (39ins) in diameter, for more than 8km (5 miles), while a B24 *Liberator* was accompanied by two red lights for 75 minutes, sometimes following, sometimes shooting ahead, manoeuvring in a way which suggested deliberate control.

Foo Fighters were seen by both night and day: they were seen coming up from the direction of the ground; they were seen with winking lights. One night fighter encountered a formation of them and decided to head straight at them. As collision seemed imminent, the lights vanished. The pilot reported: 'As I passed where they had been, I'll swear I felt the propellor backwash of invisible planes.' A few minutes later they reappeared about 825m (900yd) behind him; he decided to try to trick them, and flew into a bank of cloud, glided down for about 550m (1800ft), then reversed direction and emerged from the cloud bank at the lower height; a short while later he saw the lights emerge from the cloud bank in the opposite direction.

Whatever happened to the Foo Fighters? After their debut over the Rhineland they migrated to the Pacific: so far as is known, they have never been seen since in quite the same form.

Ghost Rockets

9 August 1946. Laxa, Denmark. At 8 pm six persons saw an object pass over the rooftops. 'It was shaped like a nine-feet long cigar and at the nose we could see some small spheres; a bluish light was produced at the rear. No sound was heard.'

The puzzled Danes had just seen a phenomenon which was to prove as baffling a phenomenon as the Foo Fighters. The 'Ghost Rockets' of Scandinavia, too, were a short-lived phenomenon, appearing for a little more than a month then vanishing. But during those few weeks some 2000 people in

Above: *Foo Fighters tracking a B24* Liberator. *Artist's impression by Brian Withams, Artist Partners.*

Sweden, Denmark and Finland were to report seeing them.

What did they report? Objects shaped like cigars or 'seagulls without heads': no wings, though some reported small fins; about 3m (9ft) long; flying slow enough — some said about 800kph (500mph) — for the eye to follow and at an altitude of 300-1000m (1000-3300ft). Usually they flew in a straight line, but sometimes they manoeuvred and sometimes they changed direction completely.

They seemed to have no hostile intention. Occasionally one was reported exploding in mid-air, but when this happened there was no debris. The only damage that occurred was when windows were shattered. One was reported plunging into Lake Oeverkalix, in northern Sweden, but a search revealed nothing. Mostly they seemed to come from the south, but by no means always.

All the obvious explanations, such as meteors, were discounted by the astronomers. The general feeling was that they must be fired by some terrestrial power — but who, in 1947, would be firing such enormous quantities of expensive missiles into the blue, with no apparent purpose?

In the sense that they were certainly flying objects, and no less certainly unidentified, Scandinavia's Ghost Rockets are classifiable as UFOs. There may be a link with the more usual type of UFO sighting in a case which occurred in Angelholm, Sweden, in May, just before the Ghost Rocket 'bombardment' began. A man named Gösta Carlson encountered a domed disc, standing on legs and with a fin, in the woods outside the town: around it were eleven figures, human in appearance and apparently of both sexes. One of them signalled him not to come near and thinking it was some secret military operation, Carlson took himself off; later he saw the disc rise from the clearing and disappear rapidly into the sky.

As with the Foo Fighters, no explanation of the Ghost Rockets has ever been forthcoming. In each case the weight and quality of the testimony makes it indisputable that the phenomenon was a very real one — but a real *what*? And is it just coincidence that the second manifestation occurred within about a year of the first, to be followed a year later by the event which can be seen as heralding the modern UFO age?

The coming of the saucers

It was Tuesday, June 24, 1947. I was flying towards the high plateau of Mount Rainier, Washington, at approximately 9200ft [2800m]. While making a turn, a tremendously bright flash lit up the surfaces of my aircraft. I was startled. I thought I was very close to collision with some other aircraft whose approach I had not noted. I spent the next 20 to 30 seconds urgently searching the sky all around. The only plane I saw was a DC-4 far to my left and rear.

Before I had time to collect my thoughts or to find any close aircraft, the flash happened again. This time I caught the direction. I observed, far to my left and to the north, a formation of very bright objects flying very close to the mountain tops at tremendous speed.

At first I couldn't make out their shapes as they were still at a distance of over a hundred miles [160km]. I could see the formation was going to pass directly in front of me. I watched, all the time thinking I was observing a formation of jets. They numbered nine, flying diagonally in an echelon formation with a gap between the first four and the last five. What startled me most was the fact that I could not find any tails on them. I figured they must be camouflaged in some way. As closely as I could determine, this formation of strange craft was travelling in excess of 1000mph [1600kph].

I was fascinated. They didn't fly like any aircraft I had ever seen before. They flew in a definite formation, but erratically, very similar to a formation of geese, in a rather diagonal chain-like line, as if they were linked together. As I put it to newsmen, they flew like a saucer would if you skipped it across the water.

It was that last phrase the reporters caught hold of later that day, after Kenneth Arnold, an American salesman who used his private plane for business, had reported his story to the manager of the firm he worked for. It was that phrase which was splashed across newspapers throughout the world. *Flying Saucers* had been added to the language.

Arnold's sighting was not the first UFO to be seen, but it was the one which sparked off the modern UFO era. To explain why, is a matter for the crowd psychologist: it just happened to be the right event at the right time. It is also a historical fact that, from that day to this, flying saucers — or unidentified flying objects as they came to be known when it was realised that only a minority were actually saucer-shaped — have been constantly in and out of the headlines. Thanks to the widespread publicity that Arnold's story received, others who had seen unaccountable things in the sky came forward with their stories: what had till then been scattered and random reports, could now be linked together in a general, if still inexplicable, pattern.

Naturally, Arnold's story was subjected to a tremendous amount of criticism. Donald Menzel, a Harvard astronomer and the most determined of UFO sceptics, explained away the sighting by stating that it was due to snow clouds. In a later book he changed his mind and decided that what Arnold had seen had been raindrops on his cockpit window.

But Arnold was an experienced pilot; it was unthinkable that he would make so childish an error. It was his professional expertise, plus his respectable character, which made his colleagues and then the press take his report seriously. The story was published by more than 150 papers across the USA and taken up by the press round the world. It was unfortunate that his report was followed by a rush of others, some serious but a great many silly, even hysterical. As a result, his own story came to seem ridiculous, too, by association. 'If I saw a ten-storey building flying through the air,' he was later to exclaim in disgust, 'I would never say a word about it.'

Right: *Jacket for* The Coming of the Saucers, *by Kenneth Arnold, 1952. (Amherst Press, Wisconsin; Mary Evans Picture Library)*

The COMING of the SAUCERS

By Kenneth Arnold & Ray Palmer

By July the press had had enough and *Newsweek* concluded that the episode was over:

> Where the flying saucers had gone, no one knew last week and few cared. Saucer-eyed scientists blamed the whirling phenomena on (1) optical illusions followed by (2) mass suggestion. As quickly as they had arrived, the saucers disappeared into the limbo of all good hot-weather headlines.

The obituary was premature. Over the next two decades, enough books and articles on the subject of UFOs were written to fill a 400-page bibliography compiled by the Library of Congress. Today the literature of ufology would fill a fair-sized library. The day of the saucer had only just begun.

The first UFO flap

It was as though the whole world had been waiting for Kenneth Arnold to report his sighting. That report triggered off a flood of others: it was the first 'flap', as clusters of UFO reports came to be described. At last those who had seen strange things — often dated earlier than Arnold's sighting — had a frame of reference into which to fit them; a label.

It was an unfortunate label. It was not even a true one: it related to the way Arnold's objects had moved, not to their shape. But the label stuck, adding an extra dimension of foolishness to what was already sufficiently improbable.

Initially, despite a fair degree of ridicule, the main impulse was serious, and in that serious climate many interesting sightings were reported. Within a few days of the Arnold report an airforce pilot saw five or six discs flying in formation in full daylight; four other airforce officers saw a strangely zigzagging light; a Milwaukee lady saw ten objects fly over her house; an Iowa bus driver saw three more; and four Oregon motorists saw four discs in the middle of the morning. At Portland, also in Oregon, three policemen and seven others saw some discs, and a United Airlines airliner was followed by five discs at sunset for 72km (45 miles).

Policemen and airline pilots had to be taken seriously, even if they were not positively believed; but among the reports which flooded into newspaper offices during the weeks following the Arnold sighting were many which were clearly natural phenomena — and many more which were unmistakeable hoaxes. It was the pattern which was to persist for the next thirty years. And then, as now, a part of the pattern consisted of cases so confused that nobody would ever know how much was fact,

how much fiction — cases like the Maury Island sighting:

On 21 June 1947 — a few days before the Arnold sighting hit the headlines — Harold Dahl, on a patrol boat off the coast near Tacoma, Washington State, with two crewmen and his teenage son, saw six doughnut-shaped craft at an altitude of about 600m (2000ft). They came lower, and it seemed to Dahl that one of them was in trouble for it hovered overhead, then started spewing out metal and other substances, injuring the boy and killing a dog. Dahl photographed the craft before they flew off.

On his return he told his boss, Fred Crissman, about the affair: Crissman was sceptical, but went out to see for himself and not only saw the strange metal but also had a glimpse of the UFOs. Early the following morning a mysterious stranger approached Dahl: by some unknown means he appeared to know all about the affair, and warned Dahl to keep quiet about what he had seen. Dahl refused to be hushed, and told investigators what he had seen; later two airforce officers arrived, checked his story, took samples of the metal and set off back to their base. En route their plane crashed and both were killed, though two other men on the aircraft parachuted to safety.

Nothing is known of the film that Dahl took. His crewmen disappeared. Investigators found themselves harassed, their hotel room bugged. An official announcement was made that Dahl and Crissman had confessed to fabricating the whole affair in order to make money from the press, though there is no evidence that they did try to do anything of the sort. Today, after many other similarly mysterious affairs, independent investigators are taking a second look at the Maury Island case, and asking whether it was the alleged confession, rather than the original sighting, that was the fabrication. Whatever the truth of the matter, it was just the sort of muddle that, over the next thirty years, was to make the confused history of the UFO more confusing than ever.

Right: *Jacket for* Flying Saucers Come from Another World, *by Jimmy Guieu, 1956. (Hutchinson Publishing Group, London; Mary Evans Picture Library)*

Flying Saucers
come
from Another World

JIMMY GUIEU

Somebody else's secret weapons

The first thought that came to everyone's minds was that UFOs were quite simply highly sophisticated aircraft developed by some earthly government. The Americans knew they were not their own, so naturally suspected the Russians: similarly the Russians suspected the Americans. It was reckoned, reasonably enough, that no other nations would have either the knowhow or the financial resources to develop such devices.

Nevertheless, America and Russia were not the only runners in the race. For centuries, Tibet has been associated with the paranormal; many people believe that mysterious beings called Bodhisattvas sit biding their time in the Himalayan fastnesses, sources of wisdom and power. These beings are normally associated with moral teachings, and occasionally with demonstrations of psychic ability, but they would not as a rule have anything to do with anything so mundane as UFOs. However, it is suggested that the eastern masters, alarmed by the runaway development of western science, may have lowered themselves to the manufacture of UFOs as a way of showing us how much greater their wisdom is than ours. If so, they have chosen a roundabout way of going about it, and not a very successful one either since the point seems to have been taken by only a few initiates.

A more credible suggestion — because the circumstantial evidence is, at least at first sight, rather appealing — is that UFOs are a development from the secret weapons which the Germans are known to have been working on during World War II. It is a fact that several of the ultra secret designs on the Nazi drawing boards bear an astonishing resemblance to certain types of UFO. According to the champions of this theory, only the crudest of the weapons — the notorious V1 and V2 rockets — ever reached operational status; others were still in the pipeline at the end of the war. Hitler, together with other Nazi leaders, made his escape from beleaguered Berlin to Norway, where a submarine convoy carried them to the secret Antarctic base already prepared in the early 1940s for such an eventuality.

In this hidden region, which is far from being the inaccessible ice desert it is popularly supposed to be, the former Nazis — who, likewise, are not malevolent fellows as claimed by the Nürnberg trials — have committed themselves to the salvation and preservation of mankind and watch over the world with loving concern. The UFOs, by this theory, have as their mission the job of keeping surveillance over the rest of us to make sure that we do not destroy the world with our blundering science.

Well, it's a nice story. We shall be looking at the 'Antarctic Base' theory again later, in quite a different connection. Nevertheless, at least one contactee has claimed that the UFO occupants speak German, and the similarity of today's UFOs to those German blueprints continues to be, at the very least, an intriguing coincidence.

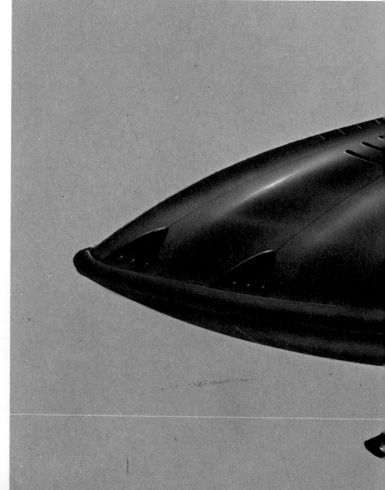

$4.95
SPECIAL OFFER

UFOs

NAZI
SECRET WEAPON?

Right: *Cover of UFOs, Nazi Secret Weapon?, by Mattern Friedrich. (Mary Evans Picture Library)*

Below: *Artist's impression of the German Model III Bellonzo-Schriever-Miethe Diskus, which is said to have achieved a speed of 2000 kph (1250 mph) at Prague on 14 February 1945. It was designed to reach speeds twice as great, and to be produced in models ranging from 45 to 75m (150 to 250ft) in diameter. (Gordon Davis, Linda Rogers Associates)*

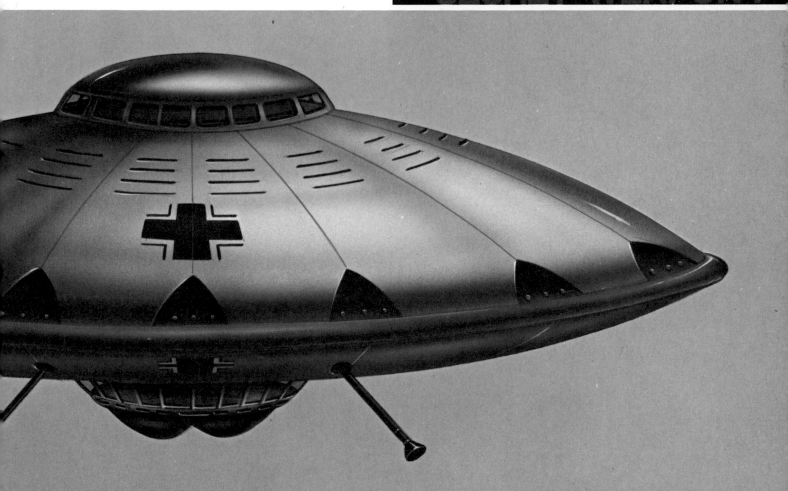

Case History:

The death of Captain Mantell

CATEGORY:	Visual/shape
PLACE:	Godman Field Air Force Base, Kentucky, USA
DATE:	7 January 1948
TIME:	1320 to 1550 hrs
WEATHER:	Bright but hazy
PERCIPIENTS:	(in air) Captain George Mantell, age 25, veteran pilot; (on ground) many airforce officers.

Just as the initial interest in UFOs was starting to fade, an event occurred which reawakened it as no other incident has done since. When an experienced airforce pilot is killed chasing a UFO, it is hard to affirm that UFOs do not exist: to say so is to say he was chasing an illusion, to which he had been directed by experienced airforce personnel, which would suggest that the entire American air defence system is incompetent. Small wonder that the Mantell incident stirred up a controversy which still rages today; while many experts consider him to have been killed while chasing a mirage, others hail him as 'ufology's first martyr'.

1 1320 hrs. Godman Field AFB receives police report that several people at Maysville, Kentucky, have seen an unusual object in the sky, estimated size 75-90m (250-300ft), described as moving 'at a pretty good clip'. Godman have no aircraft in that area and a quick check establishes that neither has any neighbouring base.

2 13.45 hrs. Godman tower sees what it assumes to be the reported object. Junior officer, reluctant to 'make a flying-saucer report', observes it for several minutes before alerting his superior. Several senior officers gather in the tower to see for themselves. Their subsequent accounts describe it as being: 'like a parachute'; an 'ice-cream cone topped with red'; 'round and white'; 'bright, disc-shaped'; 'huge and silver or metallic'; 'a small white object'; 'quarter the size of the full moon'.

3 14.30 hrs. UFO remains stationary for some 45 minutes. Four P51 *Mustangs* enter area on ferry mission. Tower requests Flight Leader Captain Mantell to check the object. One aircraft, low on fuel, lands at a neighbouring field; the three others start to climb as directed by Godman tower, not yet having a visual sighting.

4 At 3000m (10,000ft) altitude all aircraft are out of sight of Godman tower, though UFO is still visible. (Implication is that it is larger than a P51). Mantell's aircraft has pulled ahead of the others and is almost out of their sight.

Left: *Brian Withams, Artist Partners.*

5 14.45 hrs approx. Series of messages from aircraft, although their sequence is in doubt:
Mantell to tower: I see something above and ahead of me. I'm still climbing.
Wing pilot: What the hell are we looking for?
Mantell: Object is directly ahead and above and moving about half my speed . . . it appears metallic, of tremendous size.
Wing pilot: This is 15,000 feet [4500m], let's level out.
Mantell: I'm still climbing. Object is above and ahead and moving about my speed or faster. I'm trying to close in for a better look. I'm going to 20,000 feet [6000m].

6 15.20 hrs approx. By now the wing aircraft have lost both radio and visual contact with their leader, and turn back. As they pass over Godman field, one reports 'it appears like the reflection of the sun on an airplane canopy'.

7 No further report from Mantell. Though some pilots have flown above 6000m (20,000ft) for short periods without oxygen equipment, he must have known the risk. Later a friend said: 'The only thing I can think was that he was after something that he believed to be more important than his life or his family.'

8 One of the wing planes, after refuelling and taking on oxygen equipment, takes off again, climbs to 10,000m (33,000ft), scans wide area but sees nothing.

9 15.45 hrs. Mantell's plane reported crashed at Franklin, apparently after exploding in the air. No sign that Mantell attempted to get clear.

10 15.50 hrs. Godman tower loses sight of UFO.

Many suggestions were made as to what Mantell had been chasing. The astronomer Menzel offered sundogs, mock suns, but they could hardly delude an experienced flier, moving at high speeds, for half an hour or more. A more serious suggestion was the planet Venus, but experts stated that if seen at all, Venus would appear as 'an exceedingly tiny bright point of light'.

Another plausible suggestion is a government Skyhook balloon, used for meteorological purposes but not familiar to all fliers, being still classified. It is possible that a Skyhook was in the Kentucky area that afternoon, but the UFO was reported moving at speeds of 290-640kph (180-400mph).

It is reasonable to suppose that Mantell's crash was due to loss of control from oxygen starvation, caused by flying too high. But we must credit him with the sense not to go chasing after anything less than what it was said to be — an unidentified flying object, of tremendous size.

Case History:

The Adamski contact

CATEGORY:	Encounter, later boarding
PLACE:	California desert
DATE:	20 Nov. 1952 and subsequent
PERCIPIENT:	George Adamski, age 61, Polish-born restaurant employee

On a bright November day Adamski, together with his employer and a group of other friends, drove out into the California desert hoping to see UFOs. Adamski was a keen amateur astronomer and also lectured on space-age philosophy to The Royal Order of Tibet, an occult group he had formed. Aided by a telescope given him by a student, he had photographed UFOs on some 500 occasions and that day he hoped for a closer contact. He had made previous such expeditions, but in vain: he felt nevertheless that this was a likely way to encounter the objects. His faith proved justified.

Around lunchtime they reached a piece of open, rock-strewn terrain which Adamski felt was suitable. They stopped, had a picnic lunch and then, after waiting for about an hour, they saw 'a gigantic cigar-shaped silvery ship, without wings or appendanges of any kind' drifting above them. They tried to take photographs but in their excitement failed to set their cameras correctly.

Adamski had an intuition that the UFO was seeking closer contact, and asked to be driven to a less public spot: 'That ship has come looking for me, and I don't want to keep them waiting.' He was left in a remote place, just within sight of the others. The UFO had vanished, but after some five minutes there was a bright flash and he noticed a 'beautiful small craft' in the distance. He took several photographs, but unfortunately these, too, all failed to come out, except for one which shows a small and indistinct speck on the horizon.

All at once he saw a man standing about 400m (450yds) away, beckoning. He walked towards him. He turned out to be a Venusian, a little shorter than Adamski, but generally human in appearance. He appeared to be about 28 and had long, beautiful golden hair. Adamski said afterwards that 'the beauty of his form surpassed anything I had ever seen' and that he gave him 'a feeling of infinite understanding and kindness'.

The Venusian's English was scarcely better than Adamski's Venusian, but luckily they found they could communicate telepathically; indeed, they communicated so well that they were soon exchanging highly sophisticated information about what happened when Venusian reconnaissance UFOs malfunctioned in space. The two got on famously, but after nearly an hour the Venusian had to leave. Before he re-entered his spacecraft, however, he left an imprint of his foot in the desert sand, from which Adamski was able to make a cast having prudently brought plaster of Paris with him in case something of the sort should occur.

Later the imprint, which bore strange markings, was analysed by George Hunt Williamson, one of Adamski's companions on that memorable day; he extracted over sixty pages of alleged information from it. A small oval shape like a flattened O, for instance, was interpreted as representing both a UFO and an open mouth, signifying that the inhabitants of the UFO wish to speak to you — one of the simpler items!

A month later the UFO flew over Adamski's house, and the Venusian threw down a holder containing a strange photograph and a symbolic message which to this day has not been fully deciphered, though attempts to do so are still being made. Adamski was able to take some photographs of the hovering craft which came out a bit better than his previous efforts, but they were out of focus and contained no points of reference to help gauge the craft's size.

The following February, Adamski happened to be in Los Angeles, staying at a hotel, when two men came to visit him; they identified themselves as coming from Mars and Saturn. They invited him to accompany them out of town to where the Venusian scout ship was waiting, together with his Venusian friend who by now had cleverly learned to speak English fluently. It was remarkable that the two extraterrestrials found Adamski so easily, staying in a hotel, his movements unknown, particularly as neither knew him by sight.

That night he was given what he had long looked forward to — a ride in a UFO. The scout ship took him to the mother ship, where he met other extra-terrestrials, including two women 'of extraordinary beauty' who were also very friendly — one kissed him on the cheek by way of greeting. They drank and talked, but explained that they did not smoke.

Two months later he was taken on another flight, and saw the moon with the aid of a special lens in the underside of the vehicle which enabled him to observe dust, traces of vegetation and even a small furry animal. On a subsequent flight he was shown the far side of the moon where he saw towns, roads and vehicles. It is unfortunate, to say the least, that conditions on the UFO made it impossible to take any photographs, either inside the vehicle or of the scenes he could see from it. The same thing happened when they flew over Venus, whose cities 'gave me the feeling of having been transported to some wonderful fairyland.'

Many of these adventures took place before the publication of Adamski's first book, *Flying Saucers Have Landed,* but he made no mention of them for another three years until *Inside the Space Ships* was published. A cynic might feel that he had waited for the interest in the first book to die down before publishing a second and more exciting instalment — hardly the sort of behaviour to be expected from one who had been chosen, alone of all mankind, to receive such particular attentions from the ambassadors from other planets.

All who met Adamski found him quiet, dignified and courteous. Could this gentle, kindly man also be responsible for one of the greatest hoaxes that the world has ever known?

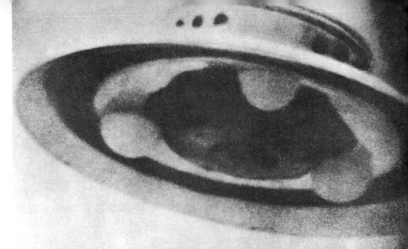

Flying Saucers Have Landed

Desmond Leslie & George Adamski

Top: *UFO photographed by Adamski in Palomar Gardens, California, on 13 December 1952. (Fortean)*

Above: *Jacket of* Flying Saucers Have Landed, *1953. (Werner Laurie, London; Mary Evans Picture Library)*

Left: *George Adamski at his telescope. (Fortean)*

Taken for a ride

Suppose you wished to discourage the King of Fiji, say, from conducting dangerous experiments with nuclear weapons which could endanger the rest of the world: would you take a small boat to land clandestinely on some unfrequented part of his coast, seek out some solitary peasant, and ask him to go to the King and persuade him to abandon his policy? Would you also give the peasant no proof of your existence, let alone your authority, to take with him, so that his only credential would be his own unsupported words?

This is, more or less, what we are asked to believe by the contactees — that curious, picturesque group of men and women (but mostly men) who claim to have been the privileged recipients of visits from other worlds, and to have been charged with a 'message to mankind' to the effect that it will go ill with us unless we give up such habits as fighting wars and experimenting with nuclear science.

Admirable sentiments, of course: one thing the UFO visitors all have in common is a benevolent attitude towards Earth, and they all display infinite friendliness towards the individuals they contact. Unfortunately they also share a dismaying impracticality in their plans to help us out with our problems. Having gone to so much trouble to send highly trained ambassadors here, their plans of action are remarkably vague. Adamski's Venusian friend spares him an hour or so of friendly chat — then has to leave. Why, where to and what for?

Logical instability is one thing that the contactees' accounts all have in common. They also share a notable absence of corroborative witness, and a reluctance on the extraterrestrials' part to supply any material souvenirs of their visit or even any dramatic new scientific data which would suggest contact with a superior technology. In short, none of the contactees who proliferated during the late 1950s in the wake of Adamski's revelations, mostly in America, give us anything that the authors of science fiction have not already given us more entertainingly.

Not that the contactees' stories are without their amusing aspects — though usually unconscious.

When Buck Nelson, a Missouri farmer who was offered a space journey to Mars one day while working in his fields, met the king of Mars, he was presented with a large Martian dog. Unfortunately, the crew of the UFO refused to have the animal inside the vehicle during the return journey, so it had to be strapped onto the outside. What everyone forgot to take into account was the effect of cosmic radiation, which caused the dog to lose much of its hair.

'There are more liars in the flying saucer field than anywhere else,' according to Kelvin Howe, who should know, having made 350 UFO journeys himself! Another veteran of many space flights, Daniel Martin of Michigan, reckoned that 'ninety-nine per cent of the other contactees are frauds'. Adamski himself, though he endorsed some of those who followed in his footsteps, reckoned that of the 3000 or so contact claims made in those years, only about 800 were valid, the others being 'merely mental experiences'. Such mutual jealousy was perhaps inevitable as the field became more crowded, but for the most part the contactees are distinguished by a refreshing kindliness and innocence.

What motivation lies behind their extraordinary claims? Somebody certainly is being taken for a ride, but who? Though some acquired a short-lived celebrity, and a few made a little money from books and lecturing, by and large the contactees made no worthwhile material gains. Rather it seems as though the phenomenon represents another aspect of that strange psychological compulsion which spurs so many people to make false confessions when a particularly sensational murder is reported by the media, or to report visions of the Blessed Virgin. It is not deliberate deceit, not calculated greed for fame or fortune — just a lonely impulse, part comic and part pathetic.

Howard Menger (born 1921) was a sign-painter until he had the experience which, though it changed his life and broke up his marriage, had the compensation of introducing him to his second wife, Marla Baxter, a beautiful Venusian who in turn informed him that he was in fact a Saturnian. His original contact had been with Marla's sister:

An opening appeared in the ship, similar to the iris of a camera. Two men got out, and then this beautiful woman stepped out and walked slowly towards me. When she came within speaking distance, she told me she was the woman I had met when I was a child. She was still the entrancing vision that I remembered; she laughed and said she was over 500 years old. . . . The meeting didn't last more than fifteen or twenty minutes — all too brief when one is conversing with an angel. . . .

Right: *Howard Menger and his Venusian wife. (Mary Evans Picture Library)*

Below: *UFO photographed by Howard Menger in the summer of 1956. (Mary Evans Picture Library)*

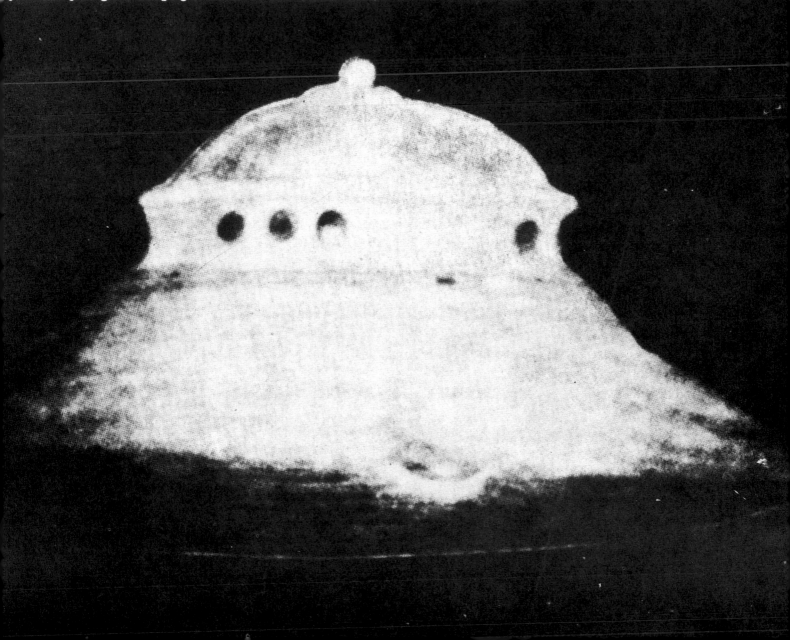

Cedric Allingham (born 1922) was an amateur ornithologist who 'met a man from another world' in the north of Scotland on 18 February 1954:

> As he advanced to meet me, I raised my arm in salute. He did the same. For a while we stood staring at each other. He, presumably, had seen other Earthmen: I had never seen a spaceman. . . What was the first essential? To find out where the man came from, undoubtedly. I pointed towards the sky and assumed a questioning attitude. The man smiled and nodded. I drew a circle to represent the orbit of Mars. I pointed to it. He nodded.

Daniel Fry (born 1908) was a rocket technician, working for Aerojet General Corporation at White Sands when on 4 July 1950 he experienced his first memorable encounter with a remote-controlled UFO, which at the time was being employed on an atmosphere-collecting operation on behalf of the mother ship hovering some 1450km (900 miles) over the earth. Walking one hot night on a desert road to get some fresh air, he came across what he realised must be a UFO; as an engineer, he was naturally curious, but when he reached out to touch the object 'a crisp voice came out of the air at my side: "Better not touch the hull, pal, it's still hot!"' The voice in fact came from a being called A-Lan, 1450km (900 miles) away in the mother ship, but he was as hospitable as though he were there on the spot:

> 'Would you like to enter the ship and perhaps make a short flight? It is only a cargo carrier with remote control, but it does have a small passenger compartment. . . If you would like a suggestion we can take you to New York City and return you here in about thirty minutes.'
>
> 'To New York — and back — in thirty minutes!' I said. 'That's eight thousand miles per hour [13,000kph]! How can you produce energies of that order on a craft like this, and how can I stand the acceleration?'
>
> 'You won't feel any ill effects,' was the reply. 'Just take a seat, and I will start the craft. I will explain some of the things which puzzle you during the ride.'

Top left: *Cedric Allingham. (Mary Evans Picture Library)*

Middle left: *UFO photographed by Cedric Allingham at Lossiemouth, Scotland, on 18 February 1954. (Mary Evans Picture Library)*

Left: *Daniel Fry. (Fortean Picture Library)*

Right: *UFO photographed by Daniel Fry at Merlin, Oregon, in May 1964. (Fortean Picture Library)*

UFOs round the world

On 26 July 1965 Latvian astronomers Robert Vitolniek, Yan Melderis and Esmeralda Vitolniek were studying noctilucent clouds at an observation station at Ogra. At 9.35 pm they noticed an unusually bright star moving slowly in a westerly direction. Looked at through x8 binoculars the 'star' resolved itself into a small, flat speck. The telescope then disclosed the following incredible picture. In the heart of a lens-shaped disc, which the astronomers estimated to be about 325 feet [100m] across, was clearly evident a thickened part, a small sphere. Around the disc, at a distance of two diameters, were three spheres resembling the one in the centre. The spheres slowly rotated around the disc as the entire system diminished in size, gradually leaving the Earth. Some 15 to 20 minutes later the spheres began to move away from the disc, as if receding in different directions. The sphere in the centre also left its place and moved away. Finally at 10 pm all these shining emerald green bodies were so far away that the astronomers lost sight of them.
(Reported in Soviet Life, *Feb 1968)*

Because so much UFO history has been transacted in the United States we tend to forget that UFOs have been seen in practically every part of the world. Some areas do seem to be more favoured than others — why are more seen over Papua, for example, than, say, Ireland? But wherever they come from, reports show that UFOs look and behave in pretty much the same way whenever they show themselves.

Below: *Crowds watch a UFO over Madrid, Spain, on 5 September 1968. (Fortean Picture Library)*

Brazil: The Trinidade Island Sighting

CATEGORY:	Shape (photographed)
PLACE:	Trinidade Island, off Brazil coast
DATE:	16 January 1958
TIME:	12.20 pm
PERCIPIENTS:	Many Brazilian naval officers and men, and Senor Barauna, photographer

The Brazilian naval vessel *Almirante Saldanha*, carrying scientists participating in the International Geophysical Year, was just about to leave the moorings where it had been for a few days when a strange 'Saturn-shaped' object flew from the direction of the Atlantic. It hovered over Desejado Peak for a few minutes, then flew away again. Though the sighting was brief and distant, the fact that it was seen by a great number of scientists and naval personnel, and photographed in front of so many witnesses, makes this one of the very best established of all UFO sightings. The diameter, height and speed of the object were estimated at 40m (130ft), 8m (26ft) and 1050kph (650mph) respectively.

Below: *UFO photographed by Senor Barauna over Trinidade Island, Brazil. (Fortean Picture Library)*

New Zealand: UFO over Dairy Farm

CATEGORY:	Near-encounter
PLACE:	Blenheim, New Zealand
DATE:	13 July 1959
TIME:	Shortly after 05.00 hrs
PERCIPIENT:	Mrs F. Moreland, cattle farmer

Mrs Moreland was up as usual at 5 am to milk her cows. She was just setting off across the frost-covered paddock to fetch the animals when she noticed a greenish glow in the clouds overhead. The glow resolved itself into two green lights which broke through the cloud and approached rapidly, lighting up everything in a bright greenish light. She hid behind a tree as the lights came to within a few paces of her. They could be seen as parts of a large flying ship — 'a large, circular, ungainly affair' — which now hovered just off the ground. It had two bands of jets round it, like sun rays, which disappeared when the machine stopped, but the bands themselves began whirling round with a low humming sound in opposite directions. Through a clear perspex top Mrs Moreland could see two figures wearing helmets, apparently dressed in silvery suits which looked like crumpled aluminium foil. She saw the rear figure stand up and examine something before him in the cabin. He then sat down again; the ship tilted slightly, the revolving bands stopped and the 'sun-ray' jets reappeared. The craft then 'shot straight up into the sky at a speed that had to be seen to be believed.'

France: The Valensole Affair

CATEGORY:	Encounter
PLACE:	Fields near Valensole, southern France
DATE:	1 July 1965
TIME:	Early morning
PERCIPIENT:	M. Masse, farmer, aged about 40

M. Masse had got up early to work in his lavender fields. He had stopped for a break near a heap of stones when he heard a whistling sound, making him think a helicopter had landed in his field. He got up and saw a strange machine about 90m (300ft)

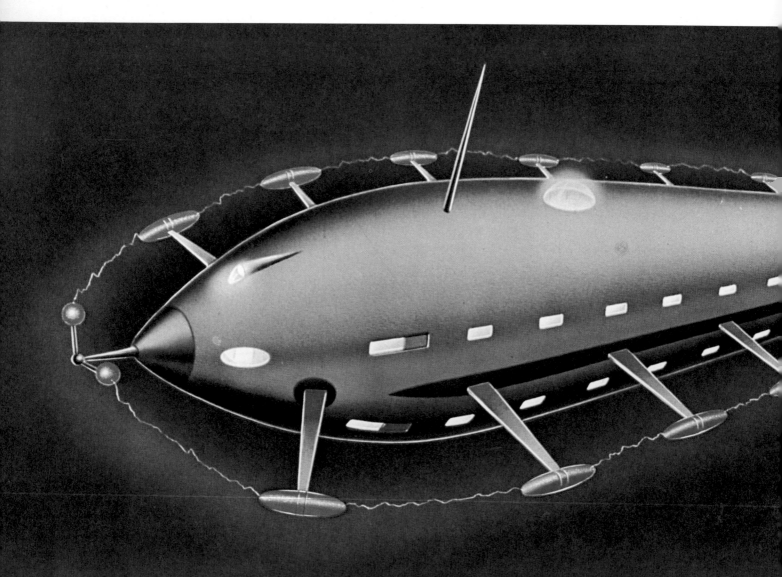

away, the shape of a rugby football, the size of a small car, standing on six legs. Two non-human figures were standing beneath it, apparently examining a lavender plant. He approached to within 6m (20ft) of them when they observed him: one made a gesture with his right hand, holding a tube-shaped object, and Masse was at once immobilised, unable to feel a thing. However, he was aware of no sense of hostility from the beings who were about one metre (39ins) high, with disproportionately large bald heads; they were dressed, and talked with a curious gurgling sound. After about four minutes the figures got into their craft through a sliding door: Masse could see them through a transparent dome. A metallic tube was drawn up from the ground into the craft which then moved backwards and away, slowly at first then more rapidly. After about 15 minutes he found he could move and he summoned the police. They and other investigators were very favourably impressed with Masse's account and his evident sincerity.

Below: Artist's impression of cigar-shaped UFO seen over Hawaii in June 1965. (Galaxy Search, Mary Evans Picture Library)

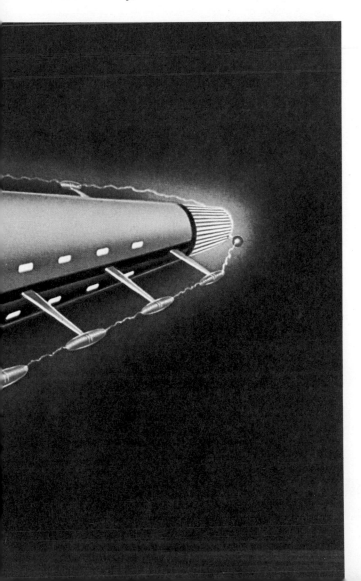

England: The Devon Police Chase

CATEGORY:	Lights
PLACE:	Near Okehampton, Devon
DATE:	24 Oct. 1967 and subsequently
TIME:	04.10 to 05.00 hrs (initial)
PERCIPIENTS.	Police constables Clifford Waycott and Roger Willey

As the two policemen were patrolling a country road they saw an unidentifiable object in the sky which seemed to move as they moved, as though deliberately pacing them. Even when they accelerated to 145kph (90mph) it kept just ahead, though never closer than about 400m (440yd). The light was not piercing, but very bright — 'star-spangled, like looking through wet glass'. It was later joined by a second object, a large cross-shaped light. The policemen chased it for 22km (14 miles) before abandoning the chase: they agreed that 'it seemed to know we were chasing it'. Their sighting was confirmed by many other reports, that night and subsequently. The calibre of the percipients resulted in wide press coverage and much speculation, but attempts to prove that the policemen were chasing either the planet Venus or an airborne refuelling exercise were simply not acceptable when set beside the reported testimony. Again, this is an unsensational case but with very good credentials.

Below: Britain's Flying Saucer Review *reports the furore created by the Devon Police Chase of October 1967. (Flying Saucer Review)*

What shape is a saucer?

We have seen how Kenneth Arnold, fumbling for a phrase to describe the way his objects moved, compared it with a saucer — and how his phrase stuck. Yet one of the most baffling aspects of the UFO problem is the astonishing variety of shapes and sizes of the things reported. It is tempting to try to reduce their number by leaving out some — the very small ones, say: but why should we assume that UFOs are built on a human scale? We have ants on earth: might not there be a planet where *all* the inhabitants are ant-sized, and their space vehicles consequently the size of a child's balloon!

On these pages are just a few of the shapes reported, each one taken from an actual sighting. One thing becomes immediately clear: very few UFOs are in fact shaped anything like a saucer. Attempts have been made to classify them, and indeed certain shapes appear to predominate. The cigar-shaped 'mother ship', usually very large and not usually seen close to earth, is one of these: it seems to have the capacity to release smaller craft — generally referred to as 'scouts' — which are vaguely disc-shaped with a dome on top. The classic Adamski photographs, whether genuine or fake, set the style for a number of later sightings: was this simple imitation, or did they all genuinely see the same type of object?

The extraordinary variety of UFO forms, though it makes our problem even more difficult, is in itself an important clue which will be taken into account when we try to assess the possible explanations.

Left: *Gordon Davis, Linda Rogers Associates*

Conspiracy?

At a certain location in space is a planet, similar to ours in most respects, whose days are numbered, for its sun is dying. Its inhabitants have searched for a suitable place to migrate to; they have picked on Earth as the most suitable, and right now they are making their preparations for the invasion. The US Government, along with that of other nations, is well aware of the situation, and is taking steps to combat it; in the meantime, to prevent world wide panic, all sightings of UFOs — which are of course reconnaissance flights from the endangered planet — are either denied or, where that is impossible, ridiculed. The FBI and CIA in America, and similar forces elsewhere, have instructions to confiscate film and other evidence, and if necessary to silence witnesses. . . .

Such is a typical example of the various conspiracy theories being voiced by those who feel there must be some sinister reality behind official reactions to UFO activity. That behaviour has been erratic and ambiguous. Individual spokesmen, sometimes claiming to represent official establishments, have uttered one-off statements: but never has there been any broad declaration of official policy. Little wonder then that many citizens, having to choose between incompetence and some more sinister motivation as the explanation for their government's attitude, have chosen the latter as more credible.

At its most extreme, the conspiracy theory involves the government in a deliberate facade of pretence. It is alleged, for instance, that in the spring of 1954 five Etherian UFOs landed voluntarily at Muroc Air Base, California. Top airforce personnel inspected them, and President Eisenhower, then golfing at Palm Springs, was flown over secretly to see the vehicles.

However, most allegations are less concrete: the government is simply accused of an almighty cover-up, of sitting on information, of calculatedly deceiving the public. The US authorities have denied any such policy, but the known involvement of the CIA and FBI in UFO investigations reveals a two-faced attitude. For lack of official guidance, individual officials have to deal with each situation as best they can — and so provide more fuel to keep the conspiracy theory bubbling.

Below left: *Dr J. Allen Hynek, eminent astronomer and chairman of the Center for UFO Studies, Evanston, Illinois. (Fortean Picture Library)*

Below: *Major Donald Keyhoe, Director of National Investigations Committee on Aerial Phenomena. (Fortean Picture Library)*

- When a searchlight, borrowed by a priest for a church fête at Norwood, Ohio, in October 1949, picked up a stationary circular object in the sky, accompanied by a number of smaller objects, is it a fact that a 4-star general drove up in a jeep and threatened to shoot the light out unless it was switched off?
- Did Fritz Werner, on 21 May 1953, assist, as he swears on oath he did, in the investigation of a crashed UFO at Kingman, Arizona, piloted by a small 4-foot creature in a silvery suit whose body Werner saw in a tent, also being examined by airforce officers?
- Was George Adamski really (as claimed) offered $35,000 if he would sign a statement to the effect that his book *Inside the Space Ships* was fiction?

In July 1952 an event at the nation's capital caused an even more alarming question to be asked. How do you react if you are the most powerful nation in the world, and your security devices indicate that aliens are intruding on the airspace over your capital city, into which not even your own aircraft are allowed to fly except by special authority?

At 21.08 hrs on 26 July 1952, for the second time in a week, radar of the Air Routes Control Center, Washington, reported between 4 and 12 unidentified blips. Two F94 jet fighters were scrambled to investigate. But New Castle AFB, Delaware, is close on 160km (100 miles) away, and nobody seemed in too much of a hurry to move. The F94s did not reach the sky over Washington until 23.25. During those 2 hrs 17 minutes the alien craft, whatever they were, had Washington at their mercy. When the fighters did reach the Washington skies, the UFOs vanished off the radar screens. When the planes turned back to their bases, the UFOs reappeared. More fighters were sent up. Lieutenant William Patterson achieved air-to-air radar contact and then a visual contact:

> I saw several bright lights. I was at my maximum speed, but even then I had no closing speed. I ceased chasing them because I saw no chance of overtaking them. I was vectored [by the ground radar] onto new objects. Later I chased a single bright light which I estimated about 10 miles [16km] away. I lost visual contact with it after about 2 miles.

In other words, not only were the security warning measures inadequate but also the counter-measures. An alarming situation? The US government was not alarmed. An intelligence chief claimed that the objects constituted absolutely no danger to the United States. Since he provided no scrap of supportive rationale for this statement, he

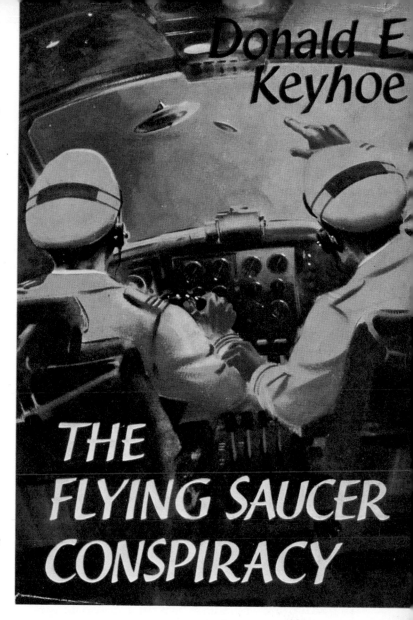

Above: *Jacket of* The Flying Saucer Conspiracy *by Major Donald Keyhoe, 1957. (Hutchinson Publishing Group, London; Mary Evans Picture Library)*

inevitably left his hearers pondering: was he speaking from ignorance or knowledge? And which was the more alarming?

In the spring of 1974 Robert Galley, French Minister of Defence, granted an interview to France-Inter Radio on the subject of UFOs. As befits a career politician, he was non-committal on the subject, but he had at least the courage to admit that a UFO problem exists: 'Among these visual phenomena we lump together under the heading UFOs, there are certainly things we don't understand. . . . If your listeners could see the quantities of reports the Gendarmerie send in, it is indeed quite disturbing.'

Which is the most disturbing: to be told your government is just as worried as you are or to be assured that there is no cause for alarm when your own eyes tell you there's every cause?

Nuts and bolts

For twenty-two years the United States Air Force, at heaven knows what cost to the American taxpayer, operated an investigative unit to collect and evaluate UFO data: ultimately it commissioned a university team, at a cost of a further $500,000, to evaluate their findings. The result was an almost completely worthless study. In 1973 one man sat down to analyse the UFO sightings in the hope that a comparative study would reveal some general patterns: James M. McCampbell's *Ufology*, the resulting study, is arguably the single most valuable piece of UFO analysis yet produced, and certainly far more useful than the $500,000 *Condon Report*.

McCampbell faces up to the fact that UFOs present science with a unique problem, in that the entire data consists of anecdotal reports by untrained observers. This it has in common with psychical research — many scientists have backed away from the UFO just as they have backed away from extra-sensory perception or from poltergeists, on the grounds that the data is inadequate — though similar considerations do not discourage them from following up equally uncertain paths in less controversial fields of study.

When the first UFO reports came in, there was little doubt in anyone's mind that they must be three-dimensional material objects which, if you could get close enough, could be touched and handled; that they moved by some kind of mechanical propulsion device and were operated by controls — in short, that they represented a form of space vehicle more advanced than our earth technology was capable of creating. If some of their characteristics seemed to defy the laws of physics as we understand them, that merely showed that those laws were not as firmly fixed as we had hoped, something the physicists were already learning.

Gradually, though, as the extraordinary range of behavioural characteristics of the UFO became apparent, many analysts gave up all hope of finding a 'nuts-and-bolts' explanation: instead they turned to thought projections, to mythological archetypes and even to occult forces of Good and Evil. Ironically, this coincided with a tendency on the part of psychical researchers to desert the mysterious darkness of the seance room for the cold light of the laboratory, finding that the new physics offers the possibility of a structural framework for their bizarre phenomena: electro-magnetic forces, for instance, seemed relevant to such manifestations as psychic healing, 'Geller' phenomena, dowsing and even the mischievous poltergeist.

In the same way, McCampbell has patiently arranged the random observations of countless UFO observers into ordered categories. What emerges is, indeed, beyond our existing technology, but not so far beyond it that we need give up all hope of finding a solution along nuts-and-bolts lines. The fundamental question, of course — and the one which, when answered, will probably help to answer all the others — is: how do UFOs escape the force of gravity? We on earth have managed it by building machines of prodigious sophistication, whose gigantic physical force enables them to fight free of gravity at enormous cost of fuel and equipment: only a tiny segment of our rockets is actually made up of the space vehicle itself. UFOs, on the other hand, have not only left wherever they came from — whether on earth or in space — but come in and out of our atmosphere as freely as birds, moving, hovering and manoeuvring as though gravity exerts no pull on them at all.

As we shall see, current theories are moving away from the outer-space hypothesis into even more remarkable areas of speculation. But simply because a UFO comes from a different plane of existence does not mean it will not possess the same physicality on its own plane as, say, our space vehicles have on ours: to transcend known laws is not to abandon all laws altogether. It still makes sense to study the nuts and bolts of ufology, even though we have to add to the control panel a switch to take us this way and that in time, or a lever to move us sideways from one universe to another.

Right: Moonship lands on Moon, *as foreseen by Chesley Bonestell in 1957, twelve years before the first moon landing. (Sidgwick & Jackson Ltd, London; MEPL)*

Case History:
Stand-off at the Kelly farmhouse

CATEGORY:	Encounter
PLACE:	Sutton Farm, Kelly, near Hopkinsville, Kentucky, USA
DATE:	21-22 August 1955
TIME:	Approx 19.00 to 03.30 hrs
PERCIPIENTS:	12 members of Sutton family and friends

The Suttons were a large family of rather poor farmers in a small rural community in Kentucky, living in a clapboard farmhouse, with electricity but few other conveniences, somewhat isolated in location. There was nothing in the history of the family or their local reputation to make deliberate lying, or fabrication caused by emotional instability, seem at all probable. Rigorous investigation tends to confirm that what the Suttons said happened *did* happen, bizarre though it was.

At about 7 pm Billy Ray Taylor, a friend of one of the Suttons, went out of the house to get a drink of water from the well; on his return he said that he had seen 'a flying saucer' land behind the farmhouse, about a city block away. Nobody took much notice, laughingly assuming that if he had seen anything at all, it had been a shooting star.

About an hour later the dog started barking, ran off and hid. One of the Suttons saw a figure approaching the house; to begin with all he could make out was 'a strange glow', then it resolved itself into 'a little man'. As described later, it was about a metre (39ins) tall, with an oversize head, very long arms and huge taloned hands; the eyes were large and glowing, and the body had a silver metal appearance. The figure approached with its hands raised in what in humans would be termed an 'I surrender' gesture — but this figure did not look human. So the two older men, Sutton and Taylor, grabbed guns and started shooting. The figure, which was then about 6m (20ft) from the house, somersaulted and vanished back into the darkness.

The two men went back into the house. A few moments later a figure — the same or another —

appeared at a window. They fired out through the screen. Again, it seemed hit and vanished. The two men went out to investigate; as they emerged, a figure on the roof reached down apparently to feel Taylor's hair. Sutton fired and knocked it over the roof. Another was spotted in a tree; it too was shot at, and seemed to be hit, but the bullets had no effect beyond driving the creature away. When another came round the corner of the house, bullets hit it with a sound like that of hitting a metal bucket. Taylor heard the shot from his .22 rifle hit one of them perched on a barrel and ricochet off: 'the little man floated to the ground and rolled up like a ball.'

By 11pm the Suttons had had enough; they all piled into the family's two cars and drove 11km (7 miles) to Hopkinsville police station. Their evident sincerity and real terror convinced the police, and within thirty minutes a considerable force had returned to Kelly. But there was no trace of the intruders: holes in the screen and cartridge cases scattered on the ground were the only evidence that anything at all had occurred. The country surrounding was extensively searched, but in vain. So, while the police tended to believe the Suttons had had a genuinely terrifying experience, there was nothing they could do; by about 2 am the police had all gone.

But was it all over? Around 3.30 am Mrs Lankford, Sutton's mother and at 50 the oldest as well as the most trustworthy of all present, was awakened to see one of the creatures staring into the bedroom. She called for help: Sutton fired at it and it vanished. It was the last the Suttons saw of their visitors.

While the Suttons' alarm is understandable, there seems no indication that their visitors had any hostile intentions: they did not retaliate in any way, and all their actions seem governed by mere curiosity. It is arguable that the Kelly fracas represents a tragically missed opportunity for a friendly confrontation.

Right: Kevin Tweddell, Artist Partners.

Hostile or friendly?

We have responded to UFOs in almost every conceivable way — complete indifference, scepticism, passionate belief, scientific curiosity, religious fervour. But astonishingly, considering what a bellicose species we are, we have rarely felt hostility towards them or feared that they intended hostility towards us. In 1967 American authors Brad Steiger and Joan Whritenour published a book entitled *Flying Saucers are Hostile,* but within a decade Steiger had changed his viewpoint dramatically, declaring that he believes 'that the UFO will serve mankind as a transformative symbol that will unite our entire species as one spiritual organism — the spiritual midwife that will bring about mankind's starbirth into the universe.'

The Kelly case exemplifies the UFOs nonaggressive attitude. Donald Hanlon has observed:

> As the first man stepped out of the door, a silvery hand reached down from the lowhanging roof and inquisitively brushed the man's hair (presumably because it lacked this feature). The 'invader' could have seriously injured the witness had it wanted to, employing its huge talons on the man's head. For this rather playful gesture the 'invader' received a volley of shotgun fire which knocked it from the roof.

The Suttons' over-reaction to their invasion can be attributed to an understandable fear of the unknown; in the same way, we may excuse some of the physical consequences that have been caused by UFOs whose occupants, in their turn, must surely feel very much on the defensive when confronted. By and large, the history of UFO visitations has been characterised by a remarkable *absence* of violence. Along with their superior technology, the UFOnauts have presumably acquired a range of defensive if not offensive weaponry; yet there are no recorded instances of such being used in any aggressive manner. The Washington UFOs made no attempt to exploit their tactical superiority.

Typical of many cases is the reaction of the French lavender farmer, M. Masse, to the beings who immobilised him in his own field, which on the

Above: *Lobby card for Eros Films'* Earth versus the Flying Saucers. *(Ronald Grant Library)*

Right: *Poster for RKO's* Killers from Space, *c. 1950. (Ronald Grant Library)*

face of it seems an unfriendly act. Interviewed on French radio, he described his feelings thus:

> When you were paralyzed by the two beings, did you feel that they were not hostile to you? No. Not a bit hostile.
> How did you feel it? By thought transmission? I can't explain it very well. I just didn't feel that they were bad, not in the least.

There are some commentators who insist that we are being lulled into a state of false security, as a prelude to invasion. Most of the early flying-saucer movies presented the UFOs as menacing; *The Day the Earth Stood Still,* however, presented the popular view that 'they' have our best interests at heart and are watching over us to make sure we do not blow ourselves to pieces with our nuclear experiments. The theme was taken up, with a much more sophisticated treatment, by the spectacular *Close Encounters of the Third Kind* which depicted a credible situation in which the aliens were seen by some to be mystic leaders and by others to be menacing foes; saviours to some, destroyers to others. Only time will tell which is the correct theory.

Mothmen and the Silver Bridge

What most ufologists would like to do would be to sit down calmly and attempt to grapple with the problem of these interesting space vehicles that appear in our skies — what form of propulsion they use, how the small scout craft are related to the larger mother ships, their electro-magnetic effects and so forth: the last thing they want is for monsters to muscle in on the act.

There is no getting away from the monsters. Like it or not, they are part of the UFO scene and too many strange creatures have been seen, in too close an association with UFOs, to be dismissed as coincidence. In the region of Newport, Oregon, over a period of several months in 1966 which were noticeable for the high number of UFOs reported in the area, more than 25 people reported seeing a giant one-eyed creature strolling round the hills. On 31 July of the same year a sixteen-year old girl in Presque Isle Park, Erie, panicked at the sight of a tall 'animated blob' — and there were eight other reports of strange creatures in the neighbourhood. On 21 July 35-year old John Osborne had seen a giant hairy creature, about 2m (6½ft) tall striding along a road in British Columbia, Canada: the next day someone else reported it; in September two girls in California described a similar creature, but a huge hunt found nothing.

On 1 September Mrs James Ikart of Scott, Mississippi, phoned the paper to report a 'man-shaped object' fluttering about the sky. Reporters found that others had seen it too. In the same neighbourhood, a few weeks later, four visitors to a wildlife park came upon a tall manlike creature with wings standing in front of an abandoned factory; on seeing the humans it waddled into the building. Within a few weeks, more than 100 people of the district — including prominent businessmen with reputations to lose, religious leaders and teachers — had all reported what became known as 'the mothman'. Their descriptions all matched: the figure was taller than a man, grey in colour, with large luminous red eyes which seemed to have a hypnotic effect. When seen in the air, mothman seemed to have wings about 3m

(10ft) in span, and to be able to fly at speeds up to 160kph (100mph). One woman recalled seeing such a creature five years before; driving with her father, she had to brake suddenly when in the middle of the highway she saw what seemed to be a very tall man in grey clothing. At a distance of about 90m (100yd) it spread a pair of wings which seemed to fill the entire breadth of the road, and zoomed straight up into the sky.

For some, mothman was a divine creature: when in March 1967 a local housewife and her daughter saw a huge creature fly across the road before them, wings outspread and white hair streaming from its head, they reported it, in terms of their own beliefs, as either Jesus or an angel.

The number of sightings built up steadily over a period of just over a year, with a noticeable concentration in a relatively small area of West Virginia. Here, at Point Pleasant, a suspension bridge known as 'the Silver Bridge' spanned the Ohio river, a vital traffic link. On 15 December, 1967, the bridge collapsed, killing 38 people. Some linked the catastrophe with an old Indian legend dating from the 1760s, which declared that certain crimes then committed by white men against the Indians would not be expiated until, after two centuries, an event would occur which would settle the score. Others linked the collapse of the bridge with the mysterious mothmen, though how these things were linked can only be guessed at.

For the serious ufologist, with quite enough problems to cope with already, mothmen and monsters are something he could do without. Unfortunately, he is not given the choice: where the UFOs go, there too, it seems, go the mothmen.

Top right: *Descriptions of today's Mothmen closely resemble these winged firemen conceived in 1900. From a card issued by a French chocolate manufacturer. (Mary Evans Picture Library)*

Right: *More sinister — and aerodynamically more credible — are the birdmen conceived by Spanish artist Francisco de Goya in his* Modo de Volar, *etched between 1819 and 1823. (Mary Evans Picture Library)*

Police report at Exeter

CATEGORY	Lights, shapes
PLACE	Exeter, New Hampshire, USA
DATE	3 September 1965 and subsequent
TIME	02.24 hrs (initial sighting)
PERCIPIENTS	Norman Muscarello, age 18, naval recruit: also two policemen and at least sixty others

'My God, I see the damn thing myself!' shouted the patrolman's voice over the police radio. Usually when a patrolman goes out to investigate a bizarre report, he finds nothing. The Exeter case was different; it started different and it went on being different.

At 2.24 am a young man burst into the Exeter police station with a wild story of how, hitchhiking home, he had seen a noiseless 'thing' come out of the sky towards him, big as a house — 25m (80ft) or

more wide — with red light pulsing round its rim. He first dived for cover, then made a run for the nearest house and pounded on the door. Nobody answered, but he flagged down a passing car which brought him into town.

A patrol car, driven by airforce veteran Bertrand, took Muscarello back to the scene to check his story. He might have refused to go if it had not been for a seeming coincidence: earlier that evening Bertrand had come across a halted motorist in a state of near-hysteria because a huge silent object, flashing red light, had followed her car just a few feet above it for several miles.

At the scene of Muscarello's sighting, Bertrand was trying to persuade the young man it had been a delusion, when it returned, bathing the entire area in a brilliant red light. Bertrand pulled Muscarello back to the car and yelled his report back to the station. Both men had the object clearly in view — about 30m (100ft) above them and a football field's length away: the brightness was too great to make out details. For a few minutes it hovered, then moved erratically away; but not before it was glimpsed by a second policeman, Patrolman Hunt, who was able to confirm what the others had seen.

If it all seemed less believable in the cold light of the following morning, the men were reassured by other reports from other sources. This, and the authority of the percipients, made it one of the most solid UFO sightings to date. Due to this fact, it came to be also one of the best reported, for it caught the attention of a professional journalist, John G. Fuller of the *Saturday Review,* who investigated the case over a period of months during which he detailed 21 separate incidents witnessed by more than 60 percipients.

Because of the police involvement, the Exeter incident was reported along official channels. No official investigation was however carried out, for it was clear to the authorities that what the policemen and Muscarello had seen was an aeroplane which they foolishly misidentified. Poor observation was thought to account for the errors regarding speed, behaviour and size. As for the other 20 reported sightings, they were considered to have been caused by weather conditions — temperature inversions which caused the illusion of disc-shaped metallic objects with flashing lights and fins — or by airforce refuelling exercises.

Uncooperatively, the policemen refused to admit that they had seen what the authorities told them they had seen. Fuller, who was totally convinced of the genuineness of the policemen's story, asserted that the government was failing in its duty by refusing to take this and similar incidents seriously. He pointed out that a high proportion of the Exeter sightings, along with many reported elsewhere, showed UFOs in close proximity to power lines; and cited the fact that UFO activity was reported on the night of 10 November, just two months later, when a still unsatisfactorily explained power failure plunged 205,000 square km (80,000 square miles) of the eastern United States and 36 million of its inhabitants into blackness, trapping 800,000 in elevator shafts, subway cars and commuter trains. Perhaps it was simple coincidence: but if there was even the slightest chance of a connection between UFOs and so major a disaster, was it not worth at least looking into?

Left: *Artist's impression of the UFO seen by Norman Muscarello and two police witnesses at Exeter, New Hampshire, on 3 September 1965. (Galaxy Search, Mary Evans Picture Library)*

The Men in Black

In September 1953 an American UFO investigator, Albert Bender, was allegedly visited by three men dressed in black. They told him that he had stumbled upon the true explanation for UFOs, but must keep it quiet: he was to close down his UFO investigation organisation and cease publication of his journal. He agreed to do so, on his honour as an American citizen, and he advised his colleagues to do the same. He was managing a motel when last heard of.

How seriously should we take Bender's story? When Bender founded his organisation, he invited all 'ardent saucer fans' to join — hardly the attitude of a scientific investigator! Again, what kind of investigator will abandon his pursuit 'on his honour as an American citizen'? A further dimension of unreality was added in 1962, when he revealed that the Men in Black had carried him in their UFO to a secret base in Antarctica, and subsequently to their home planet. His visitors, who earlier had seemed to be members of some US government establishment, were now revealed as extraterrestrials.

The verdict has to be that Bender was either lying or deluded. But his is not the only case of its kind. On 19 August 1952 a scoutmaster named Desvergers encountered a UFO in Florida. When he told of his experience, first to the police and then to airforce officials, he was informed that he had discovered the vital truth about UFOs but must keep quiet about it. 'I know what it is and it's of vital importance, but it's better for me not to go any farther for the public good,' he told reporters.

On 3 December 1953 the head of the Australian Flying Saucer Bureau, Edgar Jarrold, was visited and told to keep quiet — again, on his 'word of honour'. He was not even to pass on his knowledge to his wife. Again, one is amazed that any government or power with a vital secret should risk its discovery on the 'word of honour' of a man they hardly know. And yet, despite all these absurdities, the myth persists: there are now dozens of reports of groups of men — and just occasionally, women — dressed in black and driving smart black cars, usually Cadillacs and Lincolns in America and Rolls-Royces or Jaguars in Britain. (A delightfully surreal touch is added by reports that the cars are often of an antique model — yet *in perfect condition,* sometimes newly upholstered and smelling of that unmistakeable new-car smell!) The Men in Black always behave politely and never raise their voices or take physical action; but they are none the less menacing, having unnatural tans, awkward gaits and an apparent unfamiliarity with everyday objects.

On 11 September 1976, 58 year old Dr Herbert Hopkins, of Maine, who had been involved in hypnosis sessions with an alleged UFO contactee, received a visitor claiming to be from the New Jersey UFO Research Organisation (there is, incidentally, no such organisation). The visitor wore a black suit, black shoes, black tie, black hat and white shirt — all immaculate and creaseless. He had no hair, no eyebrows or eyelashes. He wore lipstick, and his head moved with an unnatural stiffness. He spoke in an expressionless monotone, and displayed psychic abilities — he told Dr Hopkins the contents of his pockets, and caused a coin first to change colour and then disappear, saying: 'Neither you nor anyone else on this planet will ever see that coin again'. After talking for a while about the Stephens case, he said, very slowly: 'My energy is running low — must go now — goodbye.' He walked out of the house to where Dr Hopkins could see a strange blue light, too bright for a car: both visitor and light then vanished, leaving in the driveway strange marks which had however vanished the following day. Obeying his visitor's instructions, Dr Hopkins erased his tapes and abandoned any further research in this field.

Like the mothmen, the Men in Black introduce elements into the UFO story which offend our good sense and outrage our belief. For all that, there the stories are, and they must be accounted for. Twenty five years elapsed between Bender's visit and Dr Hopkins': a myth capable of persisting that long cannot simply be ignored.

Right: *Stephen Crisp, Artist Partners.*

Two hours inside a UFO

CATEGORY:	Encounter, boarding
PLACE:	New Hampshire, USA
DATE	19 September 1961
TIME	Approx 23.00 hrs
PERCIPIENTS	Barney and Betty Hill

Barney and Betty Hill, an American couple in their forties, were driving overnight after a holiday in Canada to their home near Boston; their way took them through the hilly country of New Hampshire, along main but fairly empty roads. About 11 pm they saw a strange object in the sky which at first they assumed to be an aircraft or a satellite; when it became evident it was neither, they became curious and a little alarmed, especially as it appeared to travel along with them.

Eventually they saw it hovering beside the road, about a short city block away. Barney stopped the car and started walking across the field towards it to within some 15m (50ft), examining it through binoculars. At this distance its shape was clearly seen — a large pancake-shaped craft, with fin-like projections on either side, and a row of lit windows through which several figures could be seen. Barney could distinguish their leader, and felt that he was being willed to stop where he was. The craft came lower still, and some kind of device — possibly a ladder — was lowered from the underside.

At this point Barney panicked, ran back to the car, and drove away fast. Both he and Betty were badly scared. They became aware of a curious 'beeping' noise from the back of the car. Then they saw the lights again, and Betty said, for some reason: 'Oh no, not again'. Again they were aware of the beeping as they drove on home. Both were numbed by their experience, strangely reluctant to discuss it with each other or with anyone else. But later they felt the need to tell their story to one or two intimate friends, one of whom pointed out a strange fact: the journey had taken them at least two hours longer than it should have done. Yet the
Left: *Terry Hadler, Young Artists.*

Hills had no recollection of stopping anywhere, nor had they any distinct memory of the road for some distance after seeing the UFO. They attributed this to the queer euphoria which often overtakes night drivers: but they still felt uneasy. An experienced investigator suggested that hypnosis might help them come to terms with their experience.

What emerged from their hypnosis sessions made the Hills' story perhaps the strangest in UFO history. Each was hypnotised separately, in a series of sessions: until the end, neither heard either their own tape recordings or those of the other. Yet they added up to a consistent and amazing story. Seemingly, after Barney's precipitate return to the car, they had driven on but had taken a side turning where they came upon a group of figures standing in the road. They stopped. As if controlled in some way by the figures, the Hills got out and allowed themselves to be led away.

They were led into the woods where the UFO was standing on the ground. Inside, they were taken to separate rooms, laid on examination tables and given a medical inspection. No harm was done to them, though Barney afterwards had curious marks on his groin. The attitude of their examiners — more or less human in size and appearance — was cold but not unfriendly. After the examination they were led back to their car and told to drive on their way, having been told they would not remember what had happened. Had it not been for hypnosis, they would not have recalled the events, though Betty was plagued by nightmarish dreams in which, though she did not realise it, she was re-living the same experiences as she described under hypnosis.

Though the psychiatrist reckoned the explanation rested in an imaginary experience in Betty's mind, somehow shared telepathically by Barney, the Hills themselves found it easier to believe that their experience had actually taken place. This is supported by such details as the fact that Barney's account included details not present in Betty's. Despite its improbability, the Hills' adventure seems easier to accept as fact than as a complex psychical fabrication.

Abductions and teleportations

The Barney and Betty Hill type of case is very different from the old Adamski-style 'chosen' contact case. The 'abducted' contactees are not picked out as being special; they just stumble into their adventure. They are not rewarded with sightseeing tours of Venus or entrusted with high-flown messages to world governments: instead they are treated coldly as experimental specimens. And their stories, apart from their basic improbability, are cool, logical and consistent. It is a well-known medical fact that under hypnosis subjects become highly suggestible, often 'obliging' with fantasies to please their investigators. But the abducted-contact stories hold up well on their own and confirm one another in detail, though there is no indication that they have read one another's accounts.

Herb Schirmer
Ashland, Nebraska, USA
3 December 1967

22-year old police officer Schirmer was patrolling the streets about 2.30 am when he encountered what at first he thought to be a truck breakdown. After a closer look he returned to the station to report 'a flying saucer at the junction of Highways 6 and 63'. Then, surprisingly, he seemed to forget the experience and went home. Later, it was realised that more than twenty minutes lay unaccounted for between the sighting and his report. Like the Hills, under hypnosis he revealed that he had been taken aboard the UFO for a physical examination.

Dr and Mrs Geraldo Vidal
Argentina
May 1968

A little before midnight, Dr Vidal and his wife were driving to a party. Friends in another car were alarmed when they failed to arrive, and went back to search the road; there was no sign of them. 48 hours later, a phone call asked the friends to meet the Vidals at Buenos Aires airport. There, they told how they had driven into what seemed a patch of fog, and emerged from it to find themselves parked in an unfamiliar lane, feeling as if they had been sleeping for a long time. The car was marked as if someone had applied a blow torch to it, but was in good running order. They drove off — only to find they were in Mexico, not Argentina: they and their car had been transported, unknowingly, some 6500km (4000 miles). Dr Vidal is a well-known lawyer in Buenos Aires: their story is confirmed to the extent that another witness encountered the curious patch of fog in the same location.

John and Elaine Avis
Aveley, England
27 October 1974

The Avises, a young married couple, were driving home with their three children from a family visit when, like the Vidals, they drove into what appeared to be a bank of fog: like the Hills, they had earlier noticed a UFO close by. They were anxious to watch a television play at 10pm, but on arrival — after what should have been a 20 minute journey — they found it was 1 am: somehow they had lost three hours! Under hypnosis they revealed a story broadly similar to that told by the Hills and others, which they asserted they had never read about. Their experience was followed by a number of minor incidents — curious appearances and disappearances of household objects, a sense of being followed by certain cars, apparitions and other paranormal phenomena. At the same time, John had a breakdown and had to give up his job, eventually finding congenial work helping the mentally handicapped. He took to writing poems, gave up smoking, and became a vegetarian. And there were more sinister aspects: the police came to check on them, though the case had not been reported, and five times John was instructed to report to the police station for no known cause. As so often in ufology, one is baffled as much by the curious side effects as by the central happenings.

Right: *John Avis under examination. (Neil Breeden)*

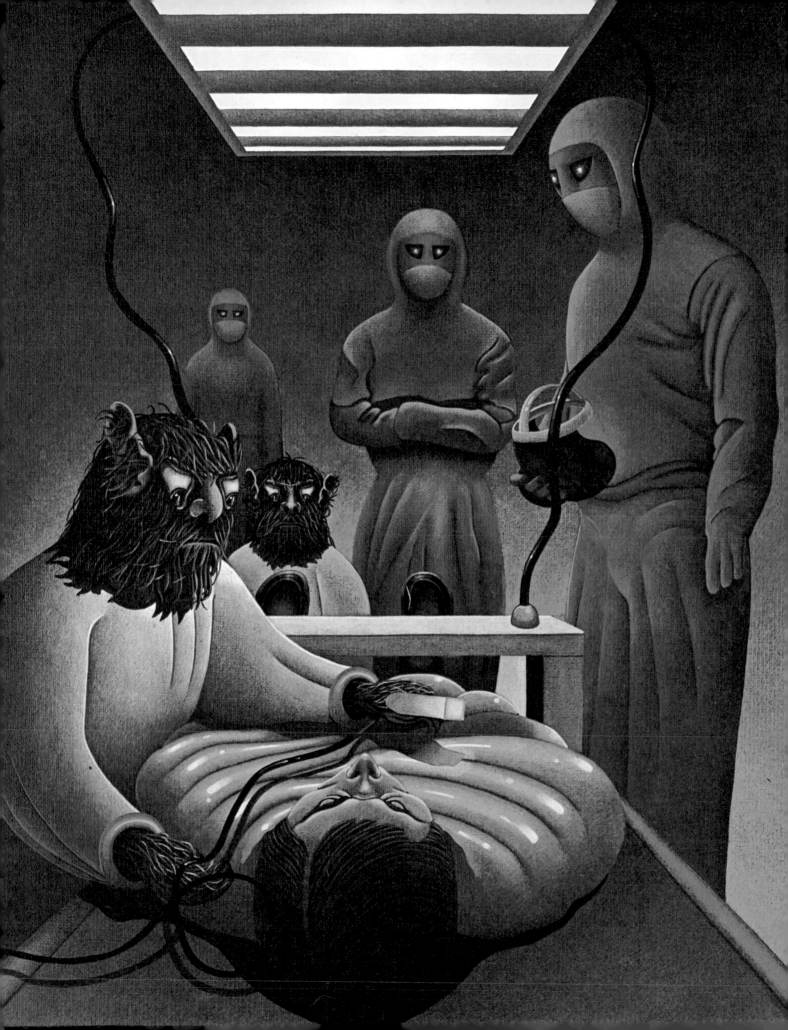

Ordinary people, extraordinary experiences

'Tuesday — Got up, went to work as usual. On way, saw UFO fly across Orchard Drive; came down on Common, saw three silvery figures emerge. After lunch . . . .' No, despite the great number of UFO sightings, they are still not everyday occurrences to be dismissed along with the other trivial happenings of the day. They continue to be something remarkable, not easy to fit in with the rest of one's experience; they leave people baffled, uneasy. When they turn to the authorities for reassurance, they generally get little sympathy unless they happen to come across someone who has had such an experience himself. Often — though not as often as previously — they are ridiculed if they tell friends or colleagues. So they tend to keep their experiences to themselves, push them to the backs of their mind and try to forget.

And yet, something extraordinary has happened to them; and there are a few who feel that the rest of the world should know what they have seen. Best of all, they would like to understand their experience; but if not, at least they may have the comfort of knowing they are not alone. So into the letterboxes of the investigation organisations and the UFO periodicals come, every day, letters from puzzled people, ordinary people who have had extraordinary experiences.

John Bracewell, a thirty-one year old quality control inspector of Manchester, England, was returning home on 21 June 1977 on his motorbike in full daylight; his wife was doing the driving and he was watching the passing townscape when he became aware of an aircraft away to their left and seemingly moving at the same speed, even slowing when they slowed. After a while he began to realise that the behaviour of the object was very unlike that of an aircraft — it was flying very low, only about three times the height of a house, and was cigar-shaped in appearance, 6-12m (20-40ft) in length, and bright silver with a dark patch in the middle. He nudged his wife to stop: when the engine was off, they realised that the UFO, too, was totally silent despite being so near. 'Why should

a UFO follow us, or more to the point, *escort* us part of the way on our journey from Manchester to Nelson and, when we stopped to watch it, give the appearance of watching us . . . Why?'

Gabriel Demoque and his girlfriend were driving on the hills near Draguignan, in southern France, on 19 October 1973, when they noticed an orange light, very bright, travelling in the sky about 600m (700yd) away. The girl became frightened, so they returned home, but Demoque and three friends, in a couple of cars, came back. They saw a strange glow and headed in its direction and parked their cars: they saw a red light approaching, heard the sound of heavy steps, and then a humanoid, some 3m (10ft) tall, emerged from the darkness. The four amateur investigators dashed back to their cars: two drove off at once, the others started downhill, then returned towards a group of approaching figures. Opening the car door, the driver shouted three times: 'Are you good or evil?' The figures seemed to be discussing among themselves; then, as they approached, the driver's nerve failed him and he drove off without ever learning the answer to his question.

Vladimir Stoicescu was just one of hundreds of citizens of Ploiesti, Romania, who on 25 August 1969 saw a large round metal object hanging over the town at lunchtime. It stayed there for some four hours, giving Stoicescu the chance to watch it closely through binoculars and also photograph it. At 1.30 the colour changed from a bright mercury to a dull metallic grey; it then proceeded to diminish in size and then split into three little spheres which later regrouped to produce another form.

On 13 April 1971 **Geoffrey Richards** and his wife, of Woodlands, West Australia, were driving early one morning when they realised they were being followed by a white light, about 60cm (2ft) in diameter. After a while it withdrew and changed to an amber glow, then changed back to white and raced up to their car at great speed, stopping only a few paces from the car at about head height: it repeated this seven more times, from behind and from the front. There was no sound at all. Evidently the object's concern was with the Richards' car: but was it, as they felt, simply tormenting them, or was there some other incalculable purpose?

On 1 January 1970 **Doreen Kendall** and **Frieda Wilson,** nurses at Cowichan District Hospital, British Columbia, Canada, were amazed to see, on pulling back the curtains of a hospital ward first thing in the morning, a large sphere hovering outside. It was about 18m (60ft) from where they stood and a further 18m (60ft) off the ground. There was a rim with lights round the sphere, which was about 15m (50ft) wide and tilted slightly in their direction, and a transparent cupola on top through which two occupants could be seen. They looked like humans and were dressed in dark

clothing. The nurses called to their colleagues; by the time they arrived the UFO had begun to move away, but it was seen clearly by many of them and one, who ran to a bathroom for a better view, saw it circle five or six times before taking off 'like a streak'.

Though far from being the most remarkable cases presented in this book, these were all unusual enough to spur their percipients into reporting their experiences: their descriptions help to build up our overall picture of the UFO, while reminding us that the great majority of UFO sightings are made by ordinary people in very ordinary circumstances.

Below: *Artist Brian James' impression of the UFO seen by Nurse Doreen Kendall at Cowichan, Canada, on 1 January 1970. From John Magor,* Our UFO Visitors, *Hancock House.*

The problem takes shape

The evidence we've looked at in the foregoing pages is just a tiny fraction of the available material: in UFOCAT, an American data bank built up by David Saunders, there are details of some 100,000 cases. Clearly, whatever they are, UFOs exist.

Equally clearly, they are an infinitely more complex phenomenon than, say, the Loch Ness 'monster'. There, the questions are fairly straight-forward: is there a monster, and if so, what is it? With the UFO we cannot reduce it to so simple a matter. Here are just some of the factors we have to consider:

1 UFOs appear to be solid, material objects, with shapes and colours that can be described; they are usually (though not always) detectable by radar. But they are able to appear and disappear at will, to hover or to move at enormous speeds, to carry out manoeuvres which are physically impossible according to earth science; and they seem to be able to change their shape (what happens to the people inside?) and to separate into smaller units or merge several into one, even at high speed. All this adds up to something technologically beyond anything we on earth are capable of.

2 UFOs are intelligently controlled. Their actions may often be hard to understand, but they seem to be purposeful. The purpose of some of them seems to be research: they have been seen apparently examining power installations; they have collected samples of soil and flowers; there are also many accounts of them examining human beings — in all, they have reacted like any normal scientist would on visiting a different planet. But this accounts for only a tiny fraction, for the majority seem to be hanging about in our skies with no discernible purpose whatever, in marked contrast to, say, our own space probes, where a massive research programme is executed with every flight.

3 A great number of UFOs are seen to contain occupants. In defiance of probability, the maj-ority are more or less human in appearance and behaviour — that is, they are more like humans than they are like anything else. Often they are able to speak our language, or to communicate telepathically. They seem to have strong mental powers, and impress human contacts with reassurance and friendliness, whether genuine or not.

4 The occupants rarely, if ever, behave in any way violent or aggressive. They seem to avoid contact with humans, except when they deliberately seek human contact on their own terms. Their apparent preference for remote districts and desert areas may be due to a desire to be inconspicuous, but it also indicates a curious lack of interest in what we consider to be our superior achievements, which one would think would excite their curiosity. Many reports, though not generally the most reliable, attribute to them a 'mission' of surveillance in our own best interests, even to the point of nominating individual humans as their representatives.

Any explanation of the UFO we come up with has got to take all of these factors into account, though some may be dismissed — thus, while admitting that the problem of the purpose of their visits is a very curious one, the 'missionary' aspect of UFO sightings seems to be highly dubious.

Dr James E McDonald, Professor of Meteorology at the University of Arizona and, until his early death, one of the best minds to grapple with the UFO problem, concluded in 1966 that the possible explanations for the UFO fell into eight categories:

1 Hoaxes, fabrications and frauds
2 Hallucinations, mass hysteria, rumour phenomena
3 Lay misinterpretations of common physical phenomena (meteorological, astronomical, optical, etc)
4 Advanced technologies (test vehicles, satellites, re-entry effect)

Above: *Fantasy — or hidden reality? (Angus McKie, Young Artists)*

5 Poorly understood physical phenomena (rare atmospheric-electrical effects, cloud phenomena, plasmas of natural or technological origin, etc)
6 Poorly understood psychological phenomena
7 Extraterrestrial probes
8 Messengers of salvation and occult truth

Even the most fervent believer in the UFO would admit that a great number of sightings have been triggered by frauds and hoaxes, and by mass suggestibility — seeing what others claim to see. Misinterpretation of physical phenomena, whether natural or artificial, must certainly account for a great many more. So without question we can write off a good many of David Saunders' 100,000 cases

to McDonald's first five categories. His eighth, though subscribed to by many contactees from Adamski onwards, lies on a different plane of discussion: we may choose to believe them or we may not. Either way, they account for only a tiny number of sightings; the vast majority of UFOs do *not* land and disgorge radiant beings with encouraging or warning messages for us earthlings.

So we are left with a short list of possible explanations — or rather, areas in which explanations may be found. In the next few pages we shall consider each in turn.

Natural phenomena?

During a heavy thunderstorm in 1920, Mr Robinson of Southport, England, was washing up the tea-things with his cousin when they saw through the kitchen window 'a big fiery ball like a football' suspended over the telephone wire which crossed the yard. Fearing an explosion, they ran out of the room; after several minutes an explosion did indeed occur, destroying a neighbour's chimney.

Reports of round glowing objects are frequent in UFO sightings, and are often very similar to the above which is an account of one of the most curious phenomena known to meteorologists — ball lightning. Disregarding the visual appearance, the behaviour — the fondness for power lines — is shared by both UFOs and ball lightning; so, though many meteorologists deny that ball lightning even so much as exists, others have chosen to see in it the explanation for many UFO sightings as well as several other curious phenomena — notably so-called spontaneous combustion, whereby people are killed by inexplicable means in closed rooms by fires which burn them up yet scarcely damage their surroundings.

It is of course tempting to use a little-known but natural phenomenon to account for another baffling phenomenon: but there are apt to be pitfalls. In this instance, we have to face the fact that ball lightning is a short-lived occurrence — generally with a life span of a few seconds, but rarely over a minute; UFOs are far more persistent. Again, the fact that ball lightning frequently causes very real damage — killing animals and people as well as destroying property — is quite at variance with the almost total harmlessness of the UFO.

And so it is with most attempts to find a natural explanation for UFOs: there tend to be as many discrepancies as there are similarities. Nevertheless, in despair of finding a nuts-and-bolts explanation, many commentators have turned to natural causes: years after his epoch-making sighting, Kenneth Arnold told a lecture audience that he thought 'they may be something alive — a living organism of some kind that can change its density'.

The leading exponent of the 'organic' theory is author Trevor James Constable, whose interest in UFOs led him to talk to some of the more way-out theorists including those who believe that the way to an explanation lies along psychic paths. Through them he came to understand that UFOs are actually life-forms in their own right, with a useful capacity for making themselves visible or invisible at will. He evolved a technique for photographing them, taking colour pictures through a filter which screens out all normal visible light, leaving only what comes into his lens at either end of the visible spectrum. By such means he obtained some curious photographs of amoeba-like creatures floating in the air, some soft like jellies, others hard like man-made objects. As far as I know, nobody else has duplicated his work, though some alleged UFO photographs do have a resemblance to his creatures.

An Austrian lady, the Countess Wassilko-Serecki, who dedicated her time and wealth to research into the paranormal, claimed to have established that some UFOs, at least, are life-forms which live in space and feed on pure energy. Normally they live in outer space, but occasionally they drop into our atmosphere. Although an interesting theory, it has no solid grounds to it and gives little help when trying to solve the UFO problem.

The history of human knowledge largely consists of transforming the unknown into the known, and we can fairly predict that many current mysteries will be explained in terms of natural extensions of present knowledge. As we learn more about electromagnetic forces, for example, it seems likely that these will help us to understand such curiosities as Geller-type spoon-bending, poltergeist phenomena and psychic healing, all of which at present tend to be accounted for in occult ways. So, in the same way, it may be found that much that is strange about the UFO will be slotted into the framework of expanding scientific knowledge. But clearly the natural explanation is quite inadequate to account for more than a tiny proportion of UFO sightings.

Right: *Ball lightning seen by Agé, near St Petersburg. From* Physique Populaire, *1888. (Mary Evans Picture Library)*

Here on earth?

'On February 18 1954 I met a man from another world'. Thus Cedric Allingham starts his account of how he met a man from Mars. But since then earthmen have sent their spaceprobes to Mars, and from their reports it is almost certain that Mr Allingham's friend must have come from somewhere else. Since they were communicating by gesture, a mistake would not be surprising.

Today most people, if asked, would opt for an extraterrestrial origin as the most likely source of UFOs. As we shall see shortly, there are substantial arguments against that idea. So it is only logical that some commentators, reluctant to go even further afield in their search, are taking a second look at the possibilities of a point of origin here on earth.

On the face of it, it seems unlikely. Most of the earth's surface has been mapped and surveyed, and is under regular observation. There are not many wildernesses or other possible hiding places left — except for one: below the surface of the earth.

Legends about a subterranean civilisation are part of the folklore of mankind. It is usually associated with evil: up is good, down is bad, in any mythology, though really there is no good reason why unless, as some suggest, the interior of the earth is peopled with malevolent beings. German ufologist August Wörner, who has a UFO study organisation near Koblenz, is convinced that UFOs come from bases deep below the earth's surface, emerging among the mountains of Tibet, which explains why that region has always been a focal point for legends about mysterious beings with superhuman powers.

True, the notion that our earth is hollow, though a myth of long standing, runs against all accepted scientific theory. But it continues to be remarkably persistent. In the early nineteenth century a distinguished American Army officer named Symmes tried to persuade Congress to finance an expedition to discover the two holes which he insisted would be found at the poles, giving access to a vast interior

Left: *Terry Hadler, Young Artists.*

region. His apparently extravagant theory was not taken seriously then, but it has recently reared its head again with satellite photos of the earth which show the polar regions as dark instead of light. There was no sign of an actual hole, admittedly, but the seeming absence of ice reminded theorists of strange stories reported by polar expeditions — of lush valleys and warm-water lakes way north of the Arctic Circle, and a warm north wind which actually causes temperatures to *rise* as you near the Pole.

In 1947 Lieutenant Commander David Bunger, flying a US naval transport plane, discovered 'Bunger's Oasis' in Antarctica — a series of warm-water lakes surrounded by ice walls: he actually landed his seaplane on one of the lakes to confirm the visual sighting. Much quoted, too, is Admiral Byrd's observation that same year, after his North Pole airborne expedition: 'I'd like to see that land beyond the pole . . . that area beyond the pole is the centre of the great unknown'. He is alleged to have flown 2700 km (1700 miles) *beyond* the pole and seen 'iceless land and lakes, mountains covered with trees, and even a monstrous animal moving through the underbrush'.

So thinly supported a claim need not be taken too seriously; but it does give the terrestrial-origin theorists room to manoeuvre. If we know so little about those areas of earth, then, yes, it *is* possible to put forward the premise that a subterranean civilisation might be alive and well and flourishing inside our earth; but to go further, to imagine it developing its technology to the point where it can produce UFOs so far ahead of our own technology, without anybody noticing — this, surely, is too fantastic to even begin to take seriously.

But then the solution, whatever it is, will have to be fantastic. Before the Men in Black persuaded him into silence, Albert Bender claimed to have solved the problem of the UFO's origin: 'I went into the fantastic and came up with the answer'. So perhaps we would do well to rule out nothing — not even the notion of a rival civilisation within our own planet.

From under the ocean?

For us humans there is a world of difference between air and water. They represent two totally contrasted environments: in one we live, in the other, unless we are careful, we die. But imagine a race of beings who found neither air nor water acceptable — or both: for them, the difference would chiefly be one of density, solved by mechanical means. For them, though underwater travel might be relatively laborious, it might also offer certain advantages: where better, for instance, to hide from man? So the possibility that UFOs operate from under the oceans has a certain logic about it — enough for the theorists to work with. Nor is it merely theory. Mysterious objects in the sea have been reported throughout history, and some at least seem to be artifacts rather than ocean monsters.

On 18 June 1845 the brig *Victoria*, becalmed in the Mediterranean, was surprised by strong gusts of wind that suddenly sprang up and battered the ship; then the wind subsided with equal suddenness, whereupon three luminous bodies rose from beneath the surface, then rose vertically into the sky until they vanished.

There have been many more recent sightings. Two Italian farmworkers in Wales at about 8 pm on 24 March 1955 saw a bright orange object, with a dark tail, dive into the sea near Rhoslefain. Almost at once it shot up again, this time leaving a grey trail behind it. Other sightings the same evening in the neighbourhood may have been of the same object.

Lakes and reservoirs are also the scene of UFO sightings. On 15 September 1962 an oval-shaped UFO was seen splashing into the reservoir at Oradely, New Jersey: soon after it took off again. On 3 June 1967, at 10 pm, a buoy tender on Lake Kipissing, Canada, saw green and white lights between two islands. Guessing that there was a boat in trouble, the tender headed towards them, and was about 30m (100ft) away when the lights rose from the water with a whooshing sound, quite different from a seaplane, and sped into the night.

Many Venezuelans believe there is a UFO base off their coast, under the waters of the Caribbean off Caracas. In March 1973 a night watchman told investigators how he had seen tubular orange lights rise out of the water and vanish in the sky: they were assured by a municipal sanitary employee that any evening between 6 and 7 pm, anybody could see — as he had seen — UFOs rising out of the water, far out at sea, and heading south at great speed. A customs officer at the airport had seen an

Left: *Barry Jackson.*

Above: *This space rocket project of 1935 startlingly anticipates today's reports of UFOs under the oceans. From* Weekly Illustrated. *(Mary Evans Picture Library)*

object glide into the sea and insisted that it was nothing like the two air crashes into the sea that he had witnessed: 'The object came down as though it was well under control and its crew were going down onto the sea-bed.'

Curiously, the existence of underwater UFO bases is confirmed by some contactee stories. Herb Schirmer, the 22-year old police officer who was taken aboard a UFO for examination, claimed to have been told that the UFOs maintained bases on earth, both underground and underwater. There was one off the coast of Florida, another off Argentina: he did not mention Venezuela, unfortunately — perhaps that one belongs to a different set of UFOs? John Avis, the Aveley contactee, made a similar report under hypnosis — his abductors told him that they maintained bases under the sea within what we term the Bermuda and other triangles.

As a source for UFOs, the oceans are definitely an outside bet: but the evidence that UFOs do make use of the waters of earth is fairly strong — and, covering as they do two-thirds of the earth's surface, they make a wonderful hiding place.

Extraterrestrial?

A visitor from Venus steps out of his spacecraft onto our Earth. Accustomed to temperatures of 400°C, he is liable to find our climate somewhat chilly; used to an atmospheric pressure nearly a hundred times as great as ours, he will find it hard to stand or move, and will feel very uncomfortable even if he doesn't actually burst; used to breathing carbon dioxide, he will hardly find our insipid atmosphere to his taste; used to thick unbroken cloud overhead he will be dazzled by the glare even on a dull earth-day; he may miss, too, the sulphuric acid and other potent chemicals he is used to taking in with every breath he takes. . . .

Such facetious objections come to mind when an Adamski claims to have encountered a visiting Venusian. There is no way in which a Venusian could adjust to earth conditions, unless our astronomers have got their facts gravely wrong. The only terms on which he could visit us is by taking a controlled environment with him wherever he goes — and staying inside it. It would be much the same with any other planet in our system; and would apply equally if we tried to visit our neighbours.

Does this mean that an extraterrestrial explanation for UFOs is totally ruled out? No, because given all the millions of millions of star systems in the universe, there are sure — statistically — to be planets where conditions are sufficiently similar to ours to make interplanetary visiting possible. But here another hurdle has to be jumped. Whereas the planets are relatively close — the journey from Venus would take only a matter of a few months — when we start to consider more distant systems we have to start thinking in terms of light years. The *nearest* possibility is 4.3 light years distant — which implies a journey more than one hundred million times the length of the moon trip of which we are all so proud: and of course the chances are that the nearest planet actually capable of making such a journey would be many times further away. In short, the extraterrestrial explanation makes sense only if we credit our visitors with having achieved what Einstein claimed to be impossible: namely, the ability to travel faster than light.

That necessarily implies a technology radically different from anything ever seriously proposed: we are in the realms of *Star Trek,* with time warps and loops to help us cross the enormous distances, with black holes providing instant tunnels through which to short-cut our journeys — imaginative concepts which may or may not have any relation to reality. But the mere fact that we can conceive of them at all, even if only as abstract possibilities, is encouraging: the history of technology demonstrates that what a man can think of, he eventually gets round to achieving.

So let us assume for the moment that UFOs are indeed from distant stars, sufficiently similar to ours for their inhabitants to feel reasonably comfortable in our atmosphere and environment, and that they have somehow conquered the inter-system travel problem. How should we expect them to behave? The reports we have of UFO behaviour, as is clear from the cases reported in this book, are puzzling and ambiguous. And those who have spoken to us have been less than enlightening.

Take the most credible, the ufonauts who borrowed police officer Herb Schirmer for twenty minutes that night in 1967. Their commander told Schirmer that he was on a four-crew observation craft, which had come from 'a nearby galaxy' (he was not saying which) inside a very much larger 'mother' ship of the traditional cigar shape. Arrived within earth's atmosphere, the mother ship functions as a base, from which the observation craft go off on their various missions. In addition, the aliens maintain base facilities underground, underwater and under the polar ice. They keep a low profile because they do not wish to disturb humanity more than they can help; they are not hostile, their purpose is purely exploratory.

Schirmer's hypnotic revelations apart, there is not a scrap of evidence to support any of this. It sounds like a human attempt to account for UFOs in human terms and according to human logic. Small wonder; it is the only logic we have, and if we

let go of it, we get lost in a labyrinth of speculation. But we will do well to bear in mind that if, even here on earth, one man's logic often seems another man's lunacy, how much more this may be the case when we are *off* the earth!

There is one other very awkward argument against the extraterrestrial thesis: the enormous number of UFO sightings. David Saunders' UFOCAT has logged some ten a day, year in and year out. Let us speculate that, at the very most, one in a hundred sightings are reported to UFOCAT, and that at best only one in ten UFOs that visit our planet are spotted by anyone at all: that makes an average of a thousand a day. Even if only one in ten of those is a genuine UFO, that is still tantamount to a hundred UFO visits a day: which must be costing somebody a lot of money with very little to show for it since most of the time, when they get here, they just hang about in the sky for us to puzzle our wits about. . . . The extraterrestrial theory may be the best theory we have, but it is a long, long way from making terrestrial sense.

Above: *UFO over the moon, as imagined by engineer Leonard Cramp in his brilliantly exploratory* Piece for a Jigsaw, *1966. (Leonard Cramp, Mary Evans Picture Library)*

All in the mind?

On 30 June 1954 Captain James Howard, flying a BOAC Stratocruiser over Labrador, observed a large dark object 'something like an inverted pear suspended in the sky' surrounded by smaller objects. They started to fly alongside the airliner, changing formation as they went. Suddenly, while Howard and his co-pilot watched, the larger object changed its shape to that of a flying arrow or delta-wing aeroplane; sometime after that it changed again, first back to a sphere and then into an elongated shape. The smaller objects then merged with it, and the entire 'thing' rapidly grew much smaller, as if moving away rapidly, became a pinpoint of light, then vanished. The UFO flew with the airliner for 130km (80 miles) during which it was seen by seven crew members as well as several passengers. 'It was a solid thing, I am sure of that,' insisted Howard.

Solid — or simply solid-seeming? The BOAC sighting, with its many experienced witnesses, is one of the best-attested on record. But was what they saw *real?* No physical object has the ability to alter its shape in that way. It is cases like this which have driven some UFO theorists to opt for a psychical explanation. They would argue that the BOAC crew only saw an illusion.

At this point you can choose between two schools of thought, depending on who is held to be creating that illusion. Is it the UFO occupants themselves, deliberately creating it? If so, you have a further choice: is there really a UFO there, and does the illusion consist only in the changing shapes? Or is there no UFO there at all — is it *all* an illusion, projected into that particular segment of sky? The recent invention of the hologram, whereby seemingly three-dimensional images can be projected into a given location in space, shows that the latter explanation is not quite as far-fetched as it sounds. Of course it still leaves the question of 'why' to be answered; was the UFO just teasing the BOAC crew to amuse itself, or was it some kind of camouflage or disguise?

The other view is that UFOs are 'created' by those who claim to see them. Ufologist David Tansley, for instance, confesses: 'Personally I have found no better explanation than the ally or composita that looks as you want it to look and acts as you expect it to behave'. Many theorists have followed in the footsteps of Carl Gustav Jung, the eminent psychologist who saw in the UFO 'a modern myth of things seen in the skies'. Drawing parallels with cultures throughout history which have looked to the skies for inspiration or instruction, for reassurance or even menace, they argue that mankind continues to look in the same direction to satisfy its psychological needs, and creates UFOs because they happen to be the appropriate symbol for our space-age mentality.

For those who are attracted by psychological theorising, the suggestion has a lot going for it, over and above the fact that it enables us to disregard so many objections which make the physical explanations so difficult to accept. Indeed, there is good reason to believe that a fair proportion of UFO sightings are no more than wish- or fear-fulfilments, longed-for saviours or terrifying bogeys, constructed by individuals to match their private hang-ups.

But there are just as many objections to the psychical theories, as becomes obvious if we apply them to the BOAC case. It is pushing such theories a bit far to suggest that Captain Howard, together with his crew and passengers, all had the same hang-ups and so all projected a thought-form of the same UFO in the same place at the same time and made it behave in the same remarkable manner. . . The theorists would have to argue that one of the witnesses did the 'creating' and somehow induced his companions into seeing it too. All this when they were supposed to be carrying out the demanding functions of a scheduled flight!

Right: *Salim Patell.*

Alternative universe?

Another universe — not out there in space, but here, where we are, invisibly interpenetrating our own universe, its atoms fitting, as it were, inside our atoms. (Remember, for all our seeming density, the fundamental units that make up our bodies are as widely separated as stars in the sky.) A universe just as real as ours, and for which our universe is as 'unreal' as theirs is for us. A universe whose existence we would never suspect were it not that, now and again, whether by accident or design, a window opens between one universe and the other, and a UFO emerges, disports itself in our atmosphere for a while, then returns as mysteriously as it came. . . .

The wildest fantasy, of course. But as each successive attempt to find an explanation for the UFO proves unsatisfactory the theorists retreat further into the unimaginable. Is this just a way of despair, taken because all the other paths are culs-de-sac? Perhaps: but it has one very practical aspect for all its fancifulness. It offers a plausible explanation to what is probably the most baffling aspect of this baffling phenomenon, the ability of the UFO to suddenly appear and equally suddenly vanish. By which we mean, not simply become invisible; that is something one might learn to do with a flick of some electro-magnetic switch. But UFOs vanish from radar screens as dramatically as they vanish from our sight: and that is a very hard trick to explain.

According to the parallel-universe theorists, UFOs dematerialize out of one universe to materialize in another — 'mat' and 'demat' are the colloquial terms for the process. Of course only one process is actually involved: our 'mat' is the other

Left: *Peter Knifton, Young Artists.*

universe's 'demat', and vice versa: it is an instant process, moreover, involving no travel in space and time except that, presumably, they have to get up off the ground of their home in that other universe in order to materialize off the ground in ours. But compared with all those light years of spaceflight which are demanded by the extraterrestrial hypothesis, that's nothing!

There are other versions. Some embody time travel instead, or in addition. The concept of time travel has been a favourite with storytellers throughout human history, and from books like Wells' *The Time Machine* it is a simple step to imagine a time traveller from some distant epoch coming to visit *us*. It has been suggested that the UFO occupants we see today are in fact tourists from the future! Perhaps this is why the UFOs maintain such a low profile and seem concerned to do nothing that will interfere with the course of things on earth — for, if they made any serious changes, that would affect the future and lead to unimaginable consequences.

Fanciful, yes: but there is one strange aspect of ufology which does seem to involve time in a curious way. It has been pointed out that several UFO manifestations involve technology just *one step ahead* of what we can currently achieve. We have seen this to be true of the American Airships of 1897; during the 1930s, strange sightings were recorded of aircraft capable of speeds and manoeuvres far beyond the capacity of the machines of the day; then in 1946 the Ghost Rockets of Scandinavia seemed to be the precursors of our space rockets; and now, when we are ourselves on the threshold of interplanetary travel, we are confronted with UFOs — once again, one step ahead, a kind of anticipation in time. Is some celestial power dangling before us spectral prototypes to encourage our inventors? Are we ourselves creating these 'previews' of what will be on the next generation's drawing boards? Or do they come from a parallel space-time continuum which just happens to be one step ahead of ours in its technical development?

Menace or miracle?

We have all seen those movies, beloved of Holly-wood, where a group of people — scientists on a life-and-death project, soldiers on a vital mission — realise that one of their party is a traitor: the cliff-hanging question is always: Which one?

That is the situation that we are in with regard to the UFO. We have looked at some of the theories about their origin: it may be presumed that one or other of them is more or less on the right lines. But while there is a certain weight of support for each

theory, there are also very grave objections — according to our present knowledge — to every one.

Since UFOs exist, it follows that somewhere, among the myriad principles which make up that present knowledge, there is an impostor. Something that we take to be so, that is not so at all. And it is that impostor which has, perhaps unwittingly, opened the door which is letting the UFOs into our skies.

But which is the impostor? Our notion of time: is

it not the absolute ruler it seems to be? According to Einstein, time too is only relative — space travellers age more slowly than those of us who stay at home. Is time our loophole?

Or space? Are we unduly impressed by those near-infinite distances that separate us from our celestial neighbours? Are there ways of reaching them as dramatically superior to our clumsy rockets as *Concorde* is to the stagecoach?

Perhaps it is more a question of something within ourselves: can we in fact do far more than we think we can? As science grapples with psychical phenomena, it is learning that the human mind really does have those remarkable powers which used to be feared as magic or dismissed as trickery. Perhaps it is here that the answer lies.

Man is pushing back the frontiers of knowledge faster now than ever in his history, and though some of us still continue to behave with appalling stupidity, as a whole the human race seems to be increasing in wisdom as well as in know-how. Many today would scorn the suggestion that the UFO has a vital part to play in that development. Yet man has always increased his knowledge by solving the problems which perplexed him: in trying to solve the problem of the UFO — surely the most perplexing phenomenon which has ever confronted man — he may have to redraft established laws of physics, rethink existing notions of space and time, make whatever changes to the structure of his knowledge that have to be made to accommodate this new phenomenon, and in so doing take a vital step forward in knowledge and understanding.

Perhaps *that* is the secret of the UFO: perhaps it is a sum scribbled on a blackboard, seemingly meaningless to our eyes, but designed by some great teacher to stretch our minds a little further?

Below: *A scene from the daringly imagined and splendidly executed climax to Columbia Pictures'* Close Encounters of the Third Kind. *(Kobal Collection)*